FINDING HOPE

A CAREGIVERS BOOK ON LOST LOVE

———— ✿ ————

NEW THINGS CAREGIVERS CAN DISCOVER
ABOUT MISSING LOVE AND REKINDLING
FEELINGS OF HOPE, HAPPINESS AND PEACE

JOHN R. RUPPEL
WITH JENNIFER ST. GILES

FINDING HOPE: A CAREGIVERS BOOK ON LOST LOVE
The Caregivers Series - Book One
Copyright © 2017 by John R. Ruppel - All rights reserved.

Editor: Jenni Grizzle
Cover Design and eBook Interior Design: Dayna Linton, Day Agency

Library of Congress Control Number: Pending

ISBN 978-0-9993448-1-1 Paperback

ISBN 978-0-9993448-0-4 e-Book

First Edition: 2017

10 9 8 7 6 5 4 3 2 1

Printed in the USA

DEDICATED TO

THIS BOOK IS THOUGHTFULLY dedicated to my wife, Wendy, without whom it would not have been possible. She has endured well her medical and other physical tests in such an admirable way, it continually motivates me.

I am deeply indebted to my five children Holly, JR, Rick, Mark and Chris for the constancy of their love and support. I am especially grateful for the edit and technical support provided by Holly, Rick and Holly's husband, Brad, who each stepped up every time I needed help or advice.

I owe a special thanks to my many grandchildren who were continually asked and pleasantly responded to help me out of many technical dilemmas. They made me feel that I was doing okay when I wondered otherwise.

This book was professionally and considerately guided by the Project Manager and publisher Dayna Linton. Her management of my bias and passion was a continual strength in the establishment of this series of caregiver books.

The editing by Jenni Grizzle was a marvel. Her innate intuition and editing excellence constantly motivated me to do it right. I was often amazed at how sensitive she was to the causes for which this book was created. I believe Jenni provided the perfect oversight for this writing.

And last, to the heroes of these books, the caregivers everywhere who labor valiantly, though often with feelings of loneliness, fatigue and frustration. It is for you these stories are presented. It is for you who are deserving of so much, that prompted these writings to tell just how deserving you really are.

TO FELLOW CAREGIVERS

YOU ARE AMONG THE ranks of a new Caregiving Generation! There are over 44 million of you actively participating as caregivers to over 60 million loved ones. That is over 100 million people in total, and millions of Millennials will soon join your ranks as they start caring for aging and ill loved ones. Your ranks do not have a dominant economic class, technical specialty, or cohesive organization, yet all of you are similarly responsible for another person's life, have daytime activities somewhat in common, and are probably doing something you've never done before.

You may not want to do what you are doing, and may even be experiencing all sorts of physical fatigue, emotional frustration, and loneliness. Yet, you continue on, possibly too tired to realize the immense impact you are having in making another human life better. The health, and well-being of a loved one hangs in the balance, and you continue on even when you find the task menacingly challenging and trying.

Much is being done for patients who have a serious illness or who have had a debilitating accident. Hospitals, nursing facilities, medical clinics, and the best physicians in the world are on duty to help your loved ones. But who is helping you? Who is providing training, information, and assistance for you?

This short-book has been created to help you with many of these needs, particularly the emotional ones. Each chapter is reader-friendly, and designed for people pressed for time, as they are divided into related topics with a focus on love, hope, and happiness. I share personal stories of real caregivers. Some of these stories are sad and tragic, and typify the pressures and frustrations of caregiving.

Contrastingly, some of these stories show how caregiving, even when difficult, can deepen love and provide a unique happiness and satisfaction. It is my hope this book will help you find those feelings on your caregiving journey.

I started research for this book because I wanted to help caregivers, like myself, find ways to care for their loved ones with serious medical conditions. I wanted to help the growing number of caregivers and their loved ones positively navigate the feelings, frustration, fatigue, and loneliness that many caregivers experience. Though initially very motivated, constant, and often long-lasting caring and sacrifice takes its toll on even the most conscientious of caregivers. Caregivers need help finding solutions and answers to their questions and needs. When caregivers neglect themselves in the situation, then the incessant duties and responsibilities of caregiving become a burden that can suffocate the love out of their relationships, including the romance they share with their spouse. This is a real danger, and its prevalence in the caretaking situation stunned me. So many people have lost hope and love. *Lost love* is the saddest casualty of the caregiving story. This short book is designed to help caregivers prevent or reverse that tragic outcome.

My wife, Wendy, and I have been through many of those same difficult moments since the time she was unexpectedly injured. Over the years, we have navigated the world of caregiving and care-receiving with our affection for one another intact. In this book, I have woven pieces of our lives with the stories of many others, so caretakers will not feel alone and can find hope to renew their energy, motivation and strength to love more.

The overriding objective is to not let obstacles keep caregivers from the nobility of their caregiving. Their influence is now and always will be critical and life-altering for the loved ones they serve. Love can be maintained in caregiving, and if absent doesn't have to remain lost.

INTRODUCTION

I RECEIVED AN UNUSUAL call one day from a retired physician friend. He began his conversation with a surprisingly direct and urgent recommendation that I do not take a planned action with my wife, Wendy. He felt it would be wrong for her and I should adopt a different course. This was totally unexpected and unsolicited on my part. But because of the urgency of his comments and my respect for him, I listened carefully. What he proposed would be difficult, with unique obstacles in its path. However, I felt he was right, and that has since been confirmed in many ways. Single-handedly, with one phone call, he changed our lives, and kept us from making a serious mistake.

The object of his phone call was to prevent our family from making a planned relocation. He feared Wendy would have a difficult adjustment to new friends and greatly miss her old ones of nearly a quarter of a century. He reminded me that if his recently deceased wife had been faced with such a move at a critical point in her life, she likely would have withdrawn and would have resisted making the sociological adjustments necessary for her recovery. He feared the same for my wife.

In my mind, I thought I knew best for my wife and could pretty much handle any complications that arose and I was somewhat taken back by his recommendation. I ended up following his advice, however, and that has since proven to be the right decision many times over again.

Wendy and I began dealing with serious medical problems when Wendy was critically injured in an automobile accident at the age of thirty. Her injuries were so severe that the medics who treated her thought she had died and delivered her to the hospital with a sheet over her head. But she was not dead, and after a month of convalescence, fighting through her many injuries, and extensive medical treatment, she returned home to begin the long, continued road to recovery.

Then came surgeries for her back, shoulders, wrists, knees (both arthroscopic and replacement), gall bladder, and five baby deliveries, eleven hospitalizations in all. She has spent her life with shoulder pain from the automobile accident, bouts with arthritis, Type 2 diabetes, a heart murmur, colitis, kidney disease and finally unexplained infections. Three times she was near death. There was more, but you get the idea. It seems like we have never been free from medical ghosts.

My personal experiences and eventual research into this caregiving crisis made me realize caregivers everywhere need someone they can speak to about the critical, time-consuming, responsibilities and the emotional stress induced upon them. They need a guideline, something that would answer caregivers' questions and help them understand the emotions involved in taking on the care of a loved one. Nearly all who attend to the medical and emotional needs of others, do so without training and are unprepared for the feelings of loneliness, inadequacy, fatigue, and despair they experience. These emotions eventually make the caregiver feel trapped, angry, and guilty.

After consulting Wendy, who in her professional life, is a family therapist, I decided to share our experience. I too have had a lot of experience counseling individuals. I have been in the hospital rooms and homes of dozens of people with serious illness, injury, or end-of-life issues. I have held the hands of many who were dying. I have felt the pain and anguish of far too many people who related that they "don't know what to do" and more commonly, "haven't ever known what to do."

So, to help caregivers who find themselves in this situation, I am sharing our story. The story of how Wendy and I ultimately found our love increasing through sharing the caregiving experience, despite all its difficulties. I hope you, too, can have such an experience.

SHORT-BOOK I
CAREGIVERS HOW-TO SERIES

LOST LOVE AND A NEW ATTITUDE

LIST OF CHAPTERS

CHAPTER 1   THE LOST LOVE
Hidden story of caregivers losing affection for loved ones

CHAPTER 2   THE RELATIONSHIP
Citing critical importance of loving, lasting relationship

CHAPTER 3   THE PROBLEM
Examines the complexity and pressures of most caregivers

CHAPTER 4   THE PATIENT
Relates the critical importance of caring for a loved one

CHAPTER 5   THE ROMANCE
Defines the importance of finding and continuing romance

CHAPTER 6   THE FORGIVENESS
The key, missing ingredient in many difficult relationships

CHAPTER 7   THE DIVORCE
Opens to view the pros and cons of ending a relationship

CHAPTER 8   THE EXPECTATIONS
Real love can motivate and possibly change everyone

CHAPTER 9   THE ULTIMATE TEST
              The key to a new way of sharing - Unconditional Love

CHAPTER 10   THE HOPE
              How hope is positive, comforting, healing and motivating

CHAPTER 11   THE HAPPINESS
              Explains how love leads to increased happiness and joy

CHAPTER 12   THE COURAGE
              Courage helps tackle starting progressing and healing

CHAPTER 13   THE SUCCESS
              Stories of getting it right and the constancy of love

CHAPTER 14   THE CONCLUSION
              Getting control of your feelings and moving forward

              THE RESOURCES
              25 Current Organizations – Local and Government

              INDEX OF REFERENCES

FINDING HOPE

A CAREGIVERS BOOK
ON LOST LOVE

———— ${\mathscr{c}}$ ————

JOHN R. RUPPEL
WITH JENNIFER ST. GILES

1.

LOST LOVE

It is not how much you do, but how much love you put in the doing.
— Mother Teresa

———————— ❦ ————————

THIS IS A STORY about love. It is a story about pain, sacrifice, despair, and those who are experiencing them. It is also a story about hope, joy, happiness, and how to achieve them. It concerns some of the most caring, and deserving people on the planet. It is a story of powerful emotion, yet tender considerations. It is a story honoring people who care and sacrifice to provide for loved ones in need.

Research reveals an increasing number of caregivers experience a reduction or full loss of love when they become the principal caregiver for a loved one. Currently, this loss of love happens to over fifty percent of those involved in caregiving situations with devastating results. Despite the caregiver's lessening affection, they carry on, doing the best they can, doing what they said they would, but they have no joy in the task. They feel burdened and guilty. Patients then feel the care they need to survive is destroying the caregiver. They feel guilty because they are a burden to the caregiver. Before examining this tragic loss, caregivers must know this unhappy, guilt-burdened cycle between caregivers and patients can be broken. (6)

Regardless of how a caregiver has been thrust into the situation, by choice or by default, they can still self-generate love for their patient. Love strengthens everyone and is the joyful path to satisfaction. Love ensures tasks are made lighter and long hours more manageable. It brings understanding, tenderness, and peace back into the caregiving equation, which results in both the caregiver and the patient feeling valued. Love is the driving emotion that makes the most difference in the attitudes, motivations and relationships of caregivers and their loved ones. And if constant, this love, becomes a life-changing force for everyone involved.

When caring for a spouse or significant other, romance is the process by which you renew your affection for the patient. If you are caring for a parent, sibling, or other, friendship is the process by which a tender and loving service can be established.

But how can a caregiver make love happen?

Let's examine some important points about this issue first:

The Hidden Story – Lost Love

IN READING THE MANY letters sent to me, I wasn't looking for nor did I expect to find, a hidden story, particularly not one so dynamic as what I found. Many, if not most, of the stories I read related the sadness the caregivers experienced because of the diminished love they felt for their loved ones. In addition, many experienced guilt at this loss of feeling. They also thought the change in their relationship as being "unavoidable." In every case, the impact of heavy labor and the unending emotional stress of their responsibility lay at the root of their loss of love. Oddly enough, they felt guilty, even though they were doing something brave and kind. (11)

Words from Alissa who feels lonely and guilty:

> *The transplant thing is torture for everyone. There are no guarantees when or if it will happen. Just a waiting game. It's very difficult to keep all of this going when there was animosity in the marriage to begin with. People get more selfish and self-absorbed as time goes on. A lot of it is fear and anger on both sides. We are just existing. Trying to find a joyful moment is hard sometimes. I miss being a real couple. My husband along with his anger and resentment, sometimes seems almost jealous that I am well. I know this is very common, I am worn out feeling guilty. He knows I am miserable. I don't know how to manage the isolation and loneliness. I try to stay positive and keep it together, but it's a losing battle.* (1)

If Love Were Lost, Where Did It Go?

THE DEGREE OF LOST love in a caregiving relationship is different for everyone. A number of letters sent to me disclosed that caretakers felt their love in the relationship with their loved one was gone. Love is an emotion of considerable substance. A commitment forged by actions over time that resides deep within our hearts. As fragile as love may seem, it is the most resilient part of the human experience. Love withstands. Love forgives. Love endures. So, I have to wonder if it is really gone in these caregiving situations. Isn't it possible, and more likely, that love has been buried by the burdens of responsibility?

Or even suppressed to gain emotional distance from the harsh realities the patient is suffering? According to marriage consultants, when faced with pain or overwhelming burdens, love can be emotionally placed in "hiding." And it will not come out of hiding unless the individual chooses to "find" it.

In some caregiving cases, the patient is uncooperative and abusive to the caregiver, seemingly doing and saying things that push the caregiver away as if he or she wants to bring an end to a relationship. That is difficult for the caregiver.

Lost love seems to be happening for this caregiver:

> *My wife has been ill for over five years. She has not yet been diagnosed. She has been to numerous doctors and no diagnosis has been found. She is in constant pain and has had to take off days from work. I, too, feel resentment, anger and guilt over having these feelings. I "should" be a loving partner and give willingly because she is my wife. I am making a life for myself but that means we do not spend much time with each other. I find it difficult to be with her and watch her suffering. I also feel angry because I blame her as well. If she ate better, if she took care of herself, then she would not be this sick. I am angry because I feel she reneged on our bargain to lead an active life. I try to be loving and take care of her but she gets angry when I offer suggestions. I go between wanting to help, to wanting to not be in this situation. I resent that this may be my life for a long time. I know we married and promised to stick together through sickness and health and want to feel loving, but we have a minimal relationship because of her debilitating situation and I am feeling less and less in love. (1)*

Physical Challenges

LET'S FACE A DIFFICULT fact. The unexpected has happened and life for both the caregiver and the patient has changed. The patient never expected to be as helpless as they are now. And the caregiver unexpectedly discovers how physically strenuous caring for another adult can be. In the beginning, love and the already established foundations of a relationship are strong enough to make the physical tasks involved in caregiving bearable. But, as time wears on, the physical strain of caregiving tasks can suffocate affections in relationships. Without enough emotional love to support the burden of his or her work, a caregiver's feelings of love erode beneath his or her growing responsibilities.

This female caregiver is suffering both mentally and physically:

> *I am exhausted mentally and physically. I feel guilty all the time for feeling angry over what our lives have come to. I am suffocating. Then the guilt sets in. I do not know how to keep living this way. There really is no conversation that does not revolve around illness. No relationship. I am desperately lonely for real male companionship. Even if I met someone, just to talk to, there is very little freedom.* (1)

Emotional Challenges

AS DIFFICULT AS THE physical challenges are, the emotional ones are even more daunting for both the patient and the caregiver. Depending upon what stage the patient is in when dealing with his illness, his emotional response can cover a wide spectrum of negative feelings before reaching a positive place. A patient's anger, frustration, depression, sense of helplessness, and guilt greatly affects a caregiver's emotional state. Ingratitude, unreturned affection, verbal abuse, and a sense of loneliness result in the caregiver feeling hopeless, forever trapped in a situation they can't avoid and can't change. In the letters I received, many caregivers said the emotional stress was greater than the physical stress. Either way, the caregivers' situations seemed impossible for them to bear. They feel like they are drowning, and no one can hear their cries for help. They feel they do not have the capacity to continue caregiving, and even more tragically, some wish they could cease living.

This caregiver is suffering loneliness, anger, guilt, frustration and depression. It is easy to feel her sadness and her "terrible dilemma."

Hi John. Like you I am a caregiver for my husband. He is dealing with kidney failure, heart failure, and limited sight due to diabetes. Like most that write on this blog, I am nurse, chauffeur, maid and everything else. Everything revolves around dialysis and doctors. Everyone seems to deal with the same issues. Loneliness, guilt, exhaustion, and depression. We all mourn for our old life, live as single people, but we are not really free. It's a terrible dilemma. Many of us are still young enough to want a full romantic life, but we can't have it. I feel constant guilt for the anger and resentment I feel. (1)

Do you feel that way? Are you emotionally challenged in your caregiving situation?

If so, you can do something about it.

Love is the most powerful emotion given to man and woman and has the greatest influence to change everything in life. When focusing on love as a positive element in a relationship instead of only seeing the negative aspects of being a caregiver, it can transform the caregiving experience. Love, when cultivated and allowed to grow, motivates and stimulates new ideas.

If you believe love is diminishing for you and your loved one in the caregiving situation, consider this idea:

Make a list of what made your life better because of your love. Is it the same now? If it is not, evaluate what has gone missing and what YOU can do about it. Then make a simple plan with several steps on how you can rebuild those elements back into your relationship with your loved one.

FINAL COMMENTS ABOUT LOST LOVE

It is hard to go back to the positive emotions and affections one felt during earlier times. Many can't or won't do it. For caregivers with a difficult physical and/or emotional trial, it feels almost impossible. Certainly, effort will be required, faith will be helpful, but choice is essential. The caregiver needs to make choices to find "lost love" no matter what it takes. That commitment will result in lost love being found. Next, I will share personal choices I made in the caregiving experience that led Wendy and me to a greater love.

2.

THE RELATIONSHIP

When you really care about someone, their happiness matters more than yours.

— curiano.com

Nine First Responders in Our Bedroom

THE MORNING DIDN'T BEGIN that way. I had, as usual, risen earlier than my wife, Wendy, and went about my morning routine. I, by chance, walked past our bedroom door to retrieve a paper I wanted to read at breakfast. The moment I heard low, mournful sounds coming from the bedroom, I knew something was wrong. I tried, but I couldn't get Wendy to respond to me. She lay there with her arm in the air pointing in the direction of the bathroom and kept moaning. I didn't know what to do about it.

Panicked, I called an emergency number, and within a few minutes two first responders arrived. Soon after, seven additional first responders arrived. All of them, all nine of them, immediately worked to save my wife. It was surreal! I hovered over them with fear drowning out my every prayer. My wife was in a deep, diabetic coma. I didn't recognize it to begin with, but as they worked, in near silence, I figured it out – Wendy was in serious trouble!

I followed the ambulance to the hospital, worried, confused, and a little out of control inside. I had never had such an experience, and I wondered what I should do. However, I was somewhat calmed by my assurance that Wendy was in good hands, and we probably acted in time to avert a tragedy. Though we had faced other personal crises together, this was the first time I had to think it through alone, and determine what to do. I found that feeling, of not knowing exactly what action to take an oppressive burden, and to this day, it occasionally haunts me.

I had to wait a long time before they let me see her, and even then, I didn't have a good answer as to what the outcome would be. She lay resting, and I remember wondering what she felt at the time. Did she know she might die? What would the effects of the – coma be? The eye-opening flood of how much I loved her overwhelmed me.

Wendy was the only woman I had ever loved, and I had to face the real possibility I could lose her. The thought devastated me. It actually physically hurt me inside. I hadn't realized the depth of my love for her even though we had been married for years. Love is affection for another that is nourished through time, and we had that. But this new flood of feeling was greater than anything I'd ever known. I wondered, did she know how much I loved her?

Maybe for the first time ever, I had come to understand what real love is. There is nothing else like it. There is no substitute for it. There is simply love. While I appreciated my new awareness, I certainly didn't want to have discovered it as I did. But I needed to discover it. And I needed to commit to showing that love to Wendy if or when I got the chance again.

Later, after Wendy recovered and our lives went back to our previous routine, I realized I had made a new commitment to our love. It is that renewed feeling and commitment that brought my attention to the loss of love so many caregivers expressed. While I don't believe I had experienced any lost love, I wanted to understand it.

I searched the Internet, urged close friends, and requested other acquaintances to write their experiences. My heart went out to caregivers who shared how difficult they found maintaining their love as the fatigue of caring for their loved one took its toll. The romantic feelings felt early in the relationship are gone. And any love they have is buried beneath the newly-acquired stress and responsibility of being a caregiver. Lost love is a tragic, collateral damage of inexperienced caregivers being thrust into the role without any education or support to deal with their situations.

Have you ever experienced the panic, the fear, the devastation of almost losing someone you love? Did you find the realization of a deeper love hidden in the pain? I did. And maybe you can find it, too.

Protect the Relationship

AFTER READING HUNDREDS OF letters, I found the negative impact caregiving had on the love and affection in the caregiving relationship alarming. The current relationship, as difficult as it might be, matters more than any of the obstacles preventing it from improving. Love is the answer. Loving is the process. Happiness for each is the ultimate reward. Love can change hearts and lives.

The story of their lost love needs to be told. I felt we needed to look at the truth of what happens and share it so other caregivers can change their own stories.

No Substitute for Love

THE GREATEST MOTIVATOR OF change is – deep, abiding, loyal love. In my research, I learned that over half of the caregiving relationships suffer loss of love. (6) The burdens of incessant duties and responsibilities in caring for another suffocate the love and romance. That finding shocked me! Although the situation mostly applies to spouses it can also apply to other care givers as well. Lost love certainly is one of the saddest casualties of caregiving!

This message of how an increase of love can change the caregivers experience and improve the loved one's health mentally if not physically is a significant one. This principle of love needs to be heard and believed, and an attitude of love must be maintained. It is the surest way to regenerate energy and service when physical tasks appear to be overwhelming. Love is what helps the caregiver keep going. It may, in many cases, be the only thing enabling the caregiver to keep going. It is probably the best possible quick fix for a weary caregiver.

Prayer Provides Strength

NO MATTER WHAT YOUR belief, praying for another develops love and empathy for them. Understand well that consideration. While the reason for the prayer might be to seek help for your injured or ill loved one, you will gain as well. By seeking help and relief for your patient, you will develop love and genuine empathy for him or her. Prayer provides strength and hope for all concerned. Prayer may take many forms and applications, but all prayers end up seeking a positive result. Seeking heavenly help for a loved one will be strengthening for all.

Open Communication

GOOD RELATIONSHIPS DON'T JUST happen. They are cultivated by considerate, prompt, and honest communication. They are best when both parties to the relationship care for one another. They are founded on patience, kindness, attention, and openness. Good communication may begin with the desire to uplift, inform, and enlighten the other party, but the most important first step is listening to and truly understanding your loved one. Be their loving, accepting friend. And remember, no one is perfect. Successful caregivers learned to be good communicators not by always saying the right thing, but by learning from their mistakes and fixing them.

Discuss Your Relationship with Your Loved One

IT IS DIFFICULT TO imagine a solid relationship without discussion. Yet, talking about relationships for some is very hard to do. That doesn't make it less important. If you want your relationship to succeed, you must tackle the hard things. But think positively about this need. Think about discussing all the things that could draw partners in any relationship closer together. To name a few: dreams, hopes, emotional and physical intimacy, attitudes, guidance, religion, use of time, children, family travel, use of money, retirement, large purchases, location of residence, love for each other, personal habits, health, living wills, conventional wills, end of life issues and many more. There is no end to important matters to be discussed, things that will bring loved ones closer together, bonding them with trust and common understanding on important issues. Speaking from experience, if it doesn't come easy at first, it still can successfully come.

Importance of Your Loved One

THE RELATIONSHIP BETWEEN THE caregiver and the loved one is paramount for a happy life: It bears repeating that relationships are perhaps the most important thing when it comes to overall life satisfaction. Having a close group of people in your life, can keep you happy for life—and help you live longer.

If you are a caregiving spouse, no relationship is more important than the one with your patient loved one. It should be cultivated like a garden growing food; food on which you are dependent for the preservation of your life. You will be happier, and your loved one will be happier, in direct proportion to the love and tender caring you provide. Happiness is earned. When happiness is earned, life gets better and longer.

Loving relationships must withstand the pressures and problems of many obstacles. Working through them is difficult, but possible.

You have read thoughts from individuals struggling with immense stress in their caregiving situations. As you read on, you will find positive stories too. And in chapter thirteen, the focus is exclusively on stories of caregivers who have dealt with, or are dealing successfully with, the trials of their responsibilities.

A suggestion for you now is to evaluate the current strengths of your relationship. How does it compare to the past? What do you feel is missing now and what needs to change? How important are those changes and when will you implement the love needed to bring those changes about? Remember, love is the key.

FINAL COMMENTS ABOUT <u>RELATIONSHIPS</u>

THE RELATIONSHIP, AS DIFFICULT as it might be, matters more than any of the obstacles preventing it from turning around and improving. Trying and doing are hard, but not reaching a loving, caregiving relationship will be a much more difficult task for a much longer time. Consistent effort will yield success. Love is the answer. Loving is the process. Happiness for all is the ultimate reward. Love and happiness can change hearts and lives—theirs and yours.

3.

THE PROBLEM

When you stop expecting people to be perfect, you can like them for who they are.
– Thatonerule.com

―――――――――― ❧ ――――――――――

Negativity

ONE OF THE MOST crucial challenges in being a principal caregiver is keeping a positive attitude. The physical and emotional pressures of providing medical care can be debilitating. Current caregivers already understand this, and new caregivers need to prepare for this. Why? Positivity is critical to having a loving relationship and maintaining the hope necessary to achieve true happiness. Also, you have decided to help your loved one, and being positive is the very best way you can do that.

Make positive decisions even when you don't *feel* positive; even when you don't *feel* cheerful; even when you no longer want to be providing care, the importance of staying positive cannot be stressed enough. Infusing your situation with the positive will be like administering a life-saving treatment to an expiring situation. Exhaustion, loneliness, discouragement and depression for the caregiver as well as the patient are eased and even sometimes eliminated by the power found in an uplifting attitude.

This act of love begins one step at a time by choosing positive thoughts over negative thoughts, or opting for the inspiring and kind response over the hurtful. Make plans for positive experiences. Search and find fun things you and your loved one can do. Look for the humor in every situation that doesn't go as expected. Share inspiring music, and find something you can both laugh about. Start each day with the thought of finding and doing one thing to make your loved one smile.

It sounds easy on paper, but it won't be easy. Yet, if you never face the caregiving responsibilities with a change for the positive in your attitude, then the situation for you and your loved one will only worsen and become more painful. Your love for this person is a good place to start, but it sometimes isn't enough. Finding outside resources to strengthen you and bring positivity to you is essential to keep your relationship going in a positive direction.

The situation may get worse before it gets better. It may never get better, but you are there to help them, and you can find a place of peace and joy in doing that no matter the outcome.

This man is struggling with being positive and ready to give up.

I'm 32 and my wife is 36. She's been battling terminal cancer for 8 years. She's spends all day in bed sleeping and never gets up except for going to chemo treatments. She doesn't even eat or drink – all nutrition is through IV. She refuses to give up and keeps

fighting. I respect her fighting but her quality of life is next to noth-
ing. She is on very high doses of pain medication and is basically
out of it all the time. She was in hospital 200 days last year and I
had to be there every day. I've haven't been to a restaurant or been
out for 2 years. I know it's very selfish but I feel like I'm suffocating
and wish for it to be over. All I want is to live like a normal person/
couple. Is that too much to ask for? I'm totally burned out and wish
to run away from the entire situation and start a new life. Right
now, it's like living life myself and I'm not allowed to go out and
enjoy life as I have to be home all the time but she can't even spend
any time with me or share anything together. (1)

Inability

WE ALL WANT TO give love, but sometimes we just can't do it. It
may be because we ourselves are not physically or emotionally able,
or it might be because our loved one's condition is simply beyond our
physical ability to make a difference. Either way, that is a very difficult
and exasperating circumstance. Medical emergencies test a relationship
differently than most other tests. The physical tasks, the necessity to
be correct and extended hours put a new and painful pressure on the
relationship.

Everyone has a breaking point. So, don't feel bad or guilty if you
have discovered yours. Most of us have never been forced to find it.
Until that moment is reached, we simply do not know how we will
react to the physical and emotional strain. In a medical emergency,
those pressures combine to create an alien setting in which we usually
struggle to adjust, and sometimes can't.

In one letter I received, a caregiver feels he's lost the ability to adjust:

Many feel that all they do is fight and they want to retire from the arena. I am struggling. My wife of 21 years, who is only 42, has suffered a brain hemorrhage. She has been in various stages of a Coma for more than 4 months now. Still not communicating, she has begun what may be a very long recovery. I still believe she will recover. I tell myself this all the time. I miss her. We have kids at home, a job, a supportive family (mine and hers), and all of this continues. Between the piles of papers in my folder just for her are everything like doctor's notes, prescriptions, approval letters, denial letters, insurance, Medicaid, disability, and bills. Wow, don't ever forget about the weight of $800,000 worth and growing, pile of bills coming in. My mind has become hazy and the days are running together. Guilty for not spending every waking moment by her side, and guilty for not letting her be and tending more to the kids. The balance is almost incomprehensible. Feelings like loneliness, sadness, confusion, fear, anger, all grazing around in my mind at one time. I will love my wife, and I will continue to be there every day as I go to the nursing home to visit. I will continue to be her best and most effective advocate for healthcare and personal care. I will continue. And I do believe that I might will keep a copy of this hidden in my underwear drawer even if I don't have the nerve to hit the "post comment" button. (1)

Unrequited

WHEN THE PATIENT DOESN'T return love and appreciation to a caregiver, it presents a very difficult and different kind of challenge for a caregiver. It really is possible for those with the illness to be kinder, more considerate, and appreciative of the care they are receiving. So, why aren't they? There are many reasons an ill loved one may be lost in this dark place of anger, unhappiness, and depression. And often, the caregiver is the only person around for the loved one to express their emotions to. Try and keep an open, non-judgmental line of communication with the loved one. Ask questions about how they feel and why. Listen to them and understand their point of view without being defensive. Maybe your loved ones just need to feel understood. Maybe they need attention that goes beyond the physical tasks of caregiving. Maybe they need a friend and feel more patience from the caregiver. Maybe they feel they are unable to love because of their illness. Counseling from a professional might help your loved ones reach a happier place in their lives.

The main thing you can do is to give love, share love, and be happy doing it every day. Not because you will get or expect anything in return, but because your love for your loved one compels you to show compassion for them. Most patients will notice your caring and loving ways and quite possibly will change. The change may come slowly, or it might not happen at all. But, in your own heart, you will know you've acted in love and can take peace and joy from that. It is the way of love!

Pain

WE ALL KNOW HOW debilitating pain can be. Pain often robs a person's ability to think or act rationally. When the nine first responders were in our bedroom, and uncertainty hovered in the air like a dark cloud, my first response was fear. After that paralyzing emotion, my fear downgraded slowly to worry, relief and then, most importantly, a flood of love. I didn't want the end of our marriage to occur in tragedy, with Wendy in a diabetic coma. I wanted her to know just how much

I loved her. And in that dire moment of great anxiety, my feelings for her strengthened me.

Once I learned she would be alright, I determined I'd make the best of that time, including doing whatever it would take every day to make her life better.

But what if I had never reached the flood of love for Wendy? What if I had gotten stuck in my fear and anxiety? I doubt we'd be at the loving, successful point in our relationship we are now. A heart filled with fear, anxiety, pain, or worry has no room for love. A heart filled with love has no place for those debilitating emotions.

Guilt

GUILT IS THE HIDDEN emotion that secretly undermines everything good in our lives. Countless letters and stories came to me, expressing the writers' guilt for feelings of lost love, or other negative thoughts and emotions they experienced from the burdens of caring for a loved one. They felt trapped and either lacked the knowledge or the courage to do anything about their situation. Usually, the caregivers were deeply troubled about losing love for their loved one. Sometimes, they had negative feelings about being lonely, fatigued, angry, or unappreciated.

First, it is important to realize loneliness, exhaustion, anger, and resentment are all real and normal emotions to have under the pressures of caring for another person day in and day out. But guilt isn't an emotion inherently tied to those negative emotions and it shouldn't be.

Caregivers caught in this reality of thinking need to take a step back. Because they are experiencing certain emotions does not mean they have committed a sin or made a tragic mistake. If this is you, then realize you have a choice. You can release guilt and grasp the courage to change your emotions by seeking ways to express and show love to your loved one. You can give up guilt. You can act with love and you will feel much better.

Note what WikiHow.com has to say about giving up guilt and moving forward:

> *"It really is a powerful moment when you see behind the simple emotion and realize that you were giving up your own power for no reason. No more feeling guilty, or at least, only for a few short moments until you discover what it's really trying to tell you. Use those emotions so you can confidently move forward."*

Hopelessness

THIS IS SO IMPORTANT, I feel I have to say it again. Hopelessness will destroy any possible future happiness in a relationship. Developing the grit to fighting through the difficulties of your situation can be done, but can only be done by you. No one else can do it for you. Life is always a struggle in one way or another. That is a fact we all need to realize, and falling into a pit of despair because of it, or because our circumstances appear so much worse than others, only steals victory away from ourselves.

This quote from the extraordinary Martha Washington captures the spirit of what I am writing this book about. *I am determined to be cheerful and happy in whatever situation I may find myself. For I have learned that the greater part of our misery or unhappiness is determined not by our circumstance but by our disposition.*

As a young man, I never considered joy or happiness could be dependent on my disposition, or, my attitude. I believed good feelings came from success, from accomplishing something important. The revelation that my disposition is key to my happiness (and also key to my unhappiness) is an important one. It deserves every caregiver's consideration.

Problems will occur. It is part of life's experience. Learning to work through the difficulties is up to us and necessary if we want more love and joy in our lives. Are you up for the challenge? Solving problems and working through the obstacles in your path can be invigorating. It provides confidence, and reminds that you are okay. We can cause change to happen. We are not trapped in a hopeless situation.

Every caregiver can enjoy the satisfaction of his or her service without losing love for the patient, even when the loved one's expectations and attitude seem unbearable. You can feel the emotional rewards of success by making a commitment to not be discouraged by the trials of your service. Make a list of your positive characteristics and qualities. Make one for your loved one, too. The positives can help see you through. Dare to believe in yourself and believe you will succeed, even if you are the only one.

FINAL COMMENTS ABOUT THE PROBLEM

IN MOST OF THE cases I studied where the caregiver had diminished love, the individual's exhaustion and fatigue had caused him to be more susceptible to negative emotions and feelings. Frequently, the comments came from caregivers who were also frustrated because they could not escape from the caregiving routine even for a short time. In their frustration, they blamed their ill loved one which resulted in a loss of love that they had no idea how to get back. Does this describe your situation? Have you realized there are answers?

4.

THE PATIENT

The best way to find yourself is to lose yourself in the service of others.
— Mahatma Gandhi

Memories Too Often Forgotten

WHEN I APPROACHED MY wife about my writing this book, or any book about caregiving, she was highly resistant. She didn't want to be projected as the patient, the spouse who needed to be only cared for and not really enjoyed. Initially that surprised me. It surprised me because she has always been independent with a strong will and seemed beyond such considerations. Although we have faced many medical issues with her health generally, it had never crippled our relationship or our friendship or our love for each other. From the very start of our marriage she stepped up and assumed her share of running our house and home. Then as time went on and I assumed more responsibilities with my career and some demanding volunteer assignments which took me out of the home many nights and on weekends, she willingly and expertly stepped up again to competently perform an even larger share of the parental duties. She never complained and thoughtfully did more than was expected. We could not have faced our many difficult family issues without her many strengths and skills. Because of her attitude and application, I never felt the emotional burdens so freely expressed by other caregivers.

This scenario correctly depicts the dilemmas of many caregivers. Burdened with the many challenges of providing service to a loved one, the immediate needs of that service tend to conceal the wonderful memories of previous years such as I have described in the previous paragraph. Well-hidden are the wonderful memories of love and cooperation made possible by my wife and the countless other spouses whose valiant and loyal service, given quietly at home, are forgotten in the caregiving crisis.

Believe the Patient Will Do Better

SO OFTEN, THE DISAPPOINTING prognosis of a physician wipes away belief that things could get better. There are enough recorded instances where, against all odds, a patient recovers. In other cases, life has been extended and health regained. Our loved ones sense our hope by the way we speak and relate to them. We must believe, in order for them to believe. For many, prayer will provide strength. For others, just believing may be enough. In any event, there is a history of miracles to read about and modern medicine makes new advances practically every day. Who is to say that this could not happen with your loved one? What amazing changes hope can bring to your caregiving situation. Hope diminishes stress and will increase health for both you and your loved one.

This lonely and frustrated woman wants to believe she can be happy:

> *I struggle with loneliness more than anything else. Our lives are all about paraplegia, dealing with cancer, and the worries that come with them. We had plans to enjoy our retirement in two years; but now he is retired on disability and I don't know when I will be able to retire. I feel guilty thinking about how my life has changed when he has lost so much. But holding my unhappiness in is not making me feel better or be a better caregiver. I want to believe that I will be happy again and enjoy life. I want to believe that I have a future. I think that would help me endure this with more grace. (1)*

Find Out What They Need

THE PATIENTS NEED TO be free to talk about their medical condition, to express their thoughts and concerns, to know someone is listening to them. So, ask them questions about what they are experiencing. But being asked the same question every day such as "how are you feeling" can feel redundant and even annoying to the patients. Ask about their progress instead. Help them start thinking about good things, about their hope, about what plans they want to make. Find out what they dream for and see if there is any way to make their hopes and dreams come true. Hope and faith in the future is possible, especially when the caregiver continually emphasizes the positive aspects of the love in one's life. The caregiver's uplifting effect will increase a patient's well-being and provide a fertile ground for love to grow.

This woman is trying to discover the needs of her husband, but keeps falling back into worry about herself and her needs:

I feel so alone. No one to turn to when there is a crisis. I worry constantly about getting sick and who will take care of my husband and dog. The day- to-day is taxing with limited sleep. Then there are days like yesterday and today that are like a living hell. Those days are the ones that are destroying me. I get so angry and frustrated I become a person I don't know and don't like. The more frustrated I get trying to get him to perform a small task the louder I talk to him, just trying to get through to him. Of course, that causes tension and he gets even more difficult and angry. I do not abuse him, but am afraid that this person I do not recognize will verbally cross that line one of these days. I pen up the anger until I break. A good cry can release quite a bit of tension. But I still hate the strange persona that is lurking in my head. You know, caregivers are giving up their lives to care for their loved ones. It is a thankless job and the only redeeming thing is that we are doing the right thing for our loved one, no matter the cost to ourselves. Some days I feel like I would rather die than face another day like today." (1)

Are you in this trap of frustration with negative emotions building to breaking levels? You can change this situation and still do the right thing for your loved one. All patients have needs and wants that are separate from their care, and a caregiver is the principal person who can see that those needs and wants are fulfilled. That doesn't mean you necessarily have to fill them, but you can find resources in the community that will. Here are some loving steps you can take:

Affection Is Important

ONE OF THE GREATEST foundations of a sweet and loving relationship is affection. It is hard to imagine a good caregiving relationship not based on sincere affection. Affection is tender, kind, loving and worthwhile. Affection is both physical and emotional. It strengthens relationships and builds happiness and joy. Affection is expressed in little things every day--a smile, a gentle touch, a flower, a back or foot rub, a treat especially prepared, remember meaningful dates and celebrating them, an unexpected outing to do something fun, even if it is only to take a drive on a sunny day.

Appreciation Is Needed

I AM OFTEN SURPRISED when my wife comments "I am so grateful for our life together" or "aren't we lucky" or compliments me for something I'd done. It usually comes at a time when I had been honestly wondering if I were doing enough, or treating her as well as I should. So, hearing her appreciation motivates me. I look for things I can compliment her about. At first, I am sorry to say I had very little practice doing this and things seemed awkward at best. But the more I complimented her, the easier it became, and the more she appreciated it. Imagine for a moment, how much your compliments can mean for your loved one. What effect could your compliments have if you recognized everything your loved one did or tried? No matter how bad you might be feeling, or how inconsiderate that person might be, or how insignificant the act, a compliment can only better the situation. Eventually, your loved one will appreciate the praise, and her heart and disposition will change.

Emotion Must Be Expressed

THE *MERRIAM-WEBSTER* DICTIONARY STATES that emotion is, "a strong feeling; excitement; having to do with the arousal of feelings." Arousal is the key word. Caregivers need to do this. There are times when deep-seated feelings have slipped away and need a new arousal. Emotion does not die, it hides, and we've already addressed a number of ways to bring love back into the caregiving situation. Now, you need to find ways to express that love to your loved one. Every person is different in what makes her feel loved by another. As a caregiver, you may think you are expressing a great deal of love in all of the things you are doing, but if patients only feels love if they get a flower or an unexpected note of love, then they won't feel they are being loved. Crazy as it is, we are all built this way.

Generosity Is Appreciated

You have not lived until you have done something for someone who can never repay you. — John Bunyan

THIS QUOTE VERY MUCH applies to the caregiving situation. This generous gifting of service and kind treatment that includes financial resources may be filling a patient's needs, but it is the caregiver who receives the ultimate blessing. The inner reward becoming love in action—for there is no greater love than to lay down one's life for another. This is what a caregiver does. So be generous in your love, not resentful. Give compliments, praise, recognition, remembrances, kindness, mercy, consistent joy and tender expressions.

Intimacy Draws You Close

I HAPPEN TO HAVE a personal advantage in regards to intimacy. While the intimacy of my own marriage has changed over the years, it is not lost. Wendy is extremely appreciative of the things I do to help her and she tries to be appropriately intimate. While I can't really empathize with those whose loved ones are critical or unappreciative, I do understand it. The need and desire for affection drives almost all relationships in the beginning. Unfortunately, the constant serving and doing for a loved one often diminishes those desires. While logic suggests serving someone should bring individuals closer together, in nearly all cases, it doesn't. Romance becomes a tragic loss in the trauma of caregiving. How can you change this reality? Make efforts to be intimate on whatever level it is possible—hold hands, have a candlelit dinner, listen to romantic music, share a dance if possible, put together a puzzle, create something together, shop on line for something you both want. Find ways and do things to remove the caregiving element from your lives for a few moments and recapture the love, intimacy and fun of the past.

Kindness Is Uppermost

CAN YOU REMEMBER HOW you were treated in the past by the person for whom you now provide care? Was that person kind and gentle with you? Were you appreciative of that kindness in those days? Did it draw you closer to that person? Do you remember how secure your loved one's kindness made you feel? If any of the answers to the above questions were yes, then evaluate how kind you should be to her now. Your kindness may be the difference in re-building a solid relationship.

But what if your relationship wasn't one of kindness before? Does that justify being unkind now? Being kind and loving now in the face of past transgressions will bring a greater love to you and your patient now.

Respect Is Bonding

DO YOU REMEMBER HOW important your loved one was to you in the past? Did you respect her? Did you show it? Did he respect you? Did he show it? Do you show the same respect to your loved one now? If not, consider revisiting the kind of respect you shared in the beginning. Even though ill, or debilitated physically or emotionally, every person is deserving of respect and consideration. How can respect be shown? First and foremost, listen to his feelings and count those feelings just as important as your own. Make even the smallest of plans and decisions together. Don't assume anything, but give your loved one the opportunity to make his own choices, even if it is inconvenient. Speak highly of your loved one to others. Respect is attitude in action.

Acknowledging what a loved one feels, enjoys, and wants is critical to your caregiving success, and expresses love and respect to him. Can you remember things said or done that made you fall in love in the first place? Can you recover anything from the past? Can you minimize present problems and begin building a new attitude and a better relationship now?

FINAL COMMENTS ABOUT PATIENTS

GOOD PERSONAL RELATIONSHIPS ARE like finding a lost treasure. They remind us what is worthwhile in life. They are valuable beyond measure, and fulfill our deepest needs and greatest dreams. They should be fought for. They should be appreciated. They should be lasting. They should be constantly enhanced and valued by everyone. In providing care to a loved one, caregivers have the unique opportunity to make that relationship their long sought- after earthly treasure.

5.

THE ROMANCE

Love is never lost. If not reciprocated, it will flow back and soften and purify the heart.
– Washington Irving

A NEW FRIEND OF mine, knowing that I was writing this book about the lost love of caregivers, suggested that I go to the New Testament of the *Bible* and look at I Corinthians 13:4. That is a verse about charity (love). It suggests that a person with charity is long suffering, is kind, it envies not, vaunteth not him or her self, and is not puffed up. I read it several times. Even after reading it several times, I still wasn't exactly sure how she thought I might use that verse.

My eyes finally fell upon the introduction to that chapter which states Charity is *"A pure love, it excels and exceeds almost all else."* Finally, I understood. Love just isn't something important, it is more important than anything else. If the author Paul is right, and I believe he is, love is to be sought for and fought for. It should be consuming, embracing, and engaging. Love should never be lost, only cherished.

In chapter nine, *The Ultimate Test*, I delve deeper into the characteristics of love. Here, I am focusing on the aspect of romance, which is the energy of love for couples and key in assuring love will not be lost in the relationship.

What Is Romance?

IS IT ONLY FOR the young and light-hearted? Can it be long lasting? Does it make life more satisfying and fulfilling? Here are some answers to those questions. Google dictionary says that romance is: "A feeling of excitement and mystery associated with love; a quality or feeling of mystery, excitement, and remoteness from everyday life." Similarly, Dictionary.com suggests that romance is: *"A love affair, an intense and happy but short-lived affair involving young people. It is romantic love idealized for its purity or beauty. It is a spirit of inclination for adventure, mystery and excitement."*

Could it be more? I truly believe so!

Love Conquers When Nothing Else Can

YOU'LL HAVE TO FORGIVE me if any of my points in this book seem repetitive. But, I truly do not think when it comes to the tragedy of loss of love, some things can't be emphasized or said enough. Whether the caregiver is in a romantic relationship such as marriage, or has been drawn into a caregiving situation without a firm foundation of love, loving kindness can still be extended. Even if the romance is a last-ditch effort to save the situation from disaster, it still has a chance, because everyone shares a driving desire to be loved. God made us that way. This is especially true between couples. We have pledged to love and cherish our partner. They need love from us, so acts of kindness and consideration are seldom refused. Continuous loving gestures can change attitudes, revitalize any situation, and strengthen a patient either physically or emotionally, or both, no matter his or her illness. For history has shown us over and over again how love conquers all obstacles. The why of this can be found in the elements of real love.

Making Hearts Happy

A FEW YEARS AGO, my granddaughter said to me, "Grandpa, you make my heart happy." I thought at the time that was a wonderful comment. I was pleased that she would say that. Then I stored her comment in my brain's memory data bank, and reflected on it briefly from time to time, pleased again each time I remembered, but never internalized it. For the purposes of this book I realize that what she said is exceptionally applicable to long-term romance. Grandparents do not judge, disapprove, scold, accuse, or ignore their grandchildren. Grandparents ask appropriate questions, and laugh considerately. Grandparents bestow gifts, affection, attention and praise. Grandparents are reliable, available, considerate and uplifting. It is no wonder that grandchildren love to share time with their grandparents – they are the object of unconditional and continual love. It occurs to me that the loving measures employed by grandparents would be similarly effective when tenderly offered to loved ones needing care. It is easy to believe that every home-bound, patient would appreciate having her caregiver "make her heart happy." After all, isn't that what romance is all about?

Committed Love (Long-term Romance)

COMMITTED LOVE IS A type of romance which is much different than the typified, madly passionate puppy love. It doesn't sparkle but for a moment here and there. Our culture does a terrible job of ever showing this except for fleeting moments like "cute old people holding hands" or in the rare example of a healthy couple on television.

Committed love is about sharing normal life together. It is about being supportive, affectionate, kind, caring, committed, responsive, and loyal. This is the stuff of the healthiest long-term couples, and can be thought of as a romance "standing in love."

Robert Johnson, a Jungian writer, calls this "stirring the oatmeal" love, and describes it as: " . . . a willingness to share ordinary human life, to find romantic meaning in the simple, unromantic tasks: earning a living, living within a budget, putting out the garbage. To 'stir the oatmeal' means to find the relatedness, the value, even the beauty in simple ordinary things, not to eternally demand a cosmic drama, an entertainment or an extraordinary intensity in everything." Some may say "that sounds so boring!" I think it's a matter of perspective. Our relationships should be a constant source of pleasure. People can have a stable relationship and an exciting life together. Go on vacation, take up new activities, explore new sexual practices, etc. Many people also get concerned when they move from romantic into committed love, and think something is "wrong" with the relationship, or that they have "fallen out of love." They often miss the opportunity for a sustainable intimate relationship, which the wise refer to as romance. (15)

No Emotion Is Stronger Than Love

THERE ARE MOMENTS IN every life more profound than others. Moments when people are called to act because of the love in their hearts. People sacrifice their lives to save another's life. Husband for wife. Wife for husband. Parent for child. Sibling for sibling. Friend for friend. Soldier for soldier. And even stranger for stranger. When God's love reigns in a person's heart, love overrides his inherent instinct of self-survival. That is a very powerful emotion. Love is stronger than any other emotion because time after time, in situation after situation, where hate, envy, resentment, hurt, anger, fear, sadness, or grief are in control, love ultimately wins over them all. No matter what situation you are called upon to face, love can only help you face and deal with the realities of caring for a seriously ill, injured, emotionally unstable or even dying loved one. I once heard it said a man considered it easier to give up his life for his wife than remember to take out the trash every week or go shopping. While that may have you smiling or shaking your head, there is some truth to the statement. A onetime decision in the middle of a crisis might be easier than a day after day, moment after moment, setting aside of your life to serve another. But the love required to make either of these sacrifices is the same. You only need to find it and tap into it.

Caution, fear can blind you from love. Fear you will fall short! Fear you are not doing enough. Or even fear you are doing too much, which will ultimately harm the wellbeing of your loved one in the future. Do your efforts seem to not be effective? Do you love the patient, but fear you are either too exhausted or too untrained to give quality care? And that hurts you terribly! Do you feel unprepared and fearful of the responsibilities thrust upon you? Does your fear make you feel guilty, and you don't know what to do about it?

Strangely enough, if you take your focus off your fears and put your focus on love, everything in your situation will change. Tender, kind, affectionate love will guide you in doing the right thing at the right time for your loved one and help you find those romantic moments you've lost. Love will help you be strong even when you feel you don't have the strength to take another step. Love will make the impossible, possible. Your task may be long lasting, but so is love.

This man loves his wife, cares for her, respects her, but still misses a loving romance. It appears that he will be constant in his care, but how tragic is the loss of romance here?

> *I am also a caregiver to my wife, who suffers from Chronic fatigue, Fibromyalgia, Parkinson's disease, and is hearing impaired. I do all the shopping and cooking and cleaning. I also have a fairly demanding job. I don't mind the cleaning and cooking, etc. And, I don't resent her. She is a kind person who was handed a bad hand of cards in life. What eats at me is the loneliness. There is no romance and I gave up trying. It is so different when you are his caretaker and nurse than when you were his sweetheart. I used to try to talk about deep things, feelings and I would hear her snoring. Life happens. I don't have the answers. I am afraid for me it is just living one day at a time and finding a moment of joy by myself, like a sunset or a good meal when I am shopping. (1)*

Is this your situation? How long can anyone last under these conditions without eventually making a bad decision to fill one's need for romance? What can help this man and you?

Love Is the Difference

I DON'T REPEAT MYSELF without purpose. Love is the one thing that can make the most difference in the attitude and motivation of caregivers and their loved ones. That kind of love, if constant, can change the life of another. But, an increasing number of caregivers, possibly like you, are experiencing a reduction or full loss of love because of their caregiving. That doesn't have to include you. Do your part to see your love is not lost in the collateral damage of caregiving. Your decision to change and demonstrate true love is a critical one.

There Is Always Room for Love

THE AVERAGE LIFE IS very full! Full of things that are important and some things that are not. These obstacles come slowly and then at some unexpected moment they may fill time and emotions. Often it will feel like nothing else can be fitted into daily routines. And then comes the moment when unavoidable tragedy or trial enters the individual's life. Now one is faced with fitting in more care giving time, more unwelcome inconvenience and more caring when it feels there is just simply no time for anything more.

Often the newest trauma deals us a serious blow. When the trauma swirls around someone we love, and we don't know what to do, we may search for other answers. In the case of my wife's diabetic coma related earlier in this short-book, that happened to me. But I found the solution to the problem, for me, was love. I determined I would be there for her no matter what was recommended by the physicians. I was not willing to end our romance. You shouldn't either.

Usually there is no choice. Most caregivers must manage to find room for love to move forward and deal with it. They focus. But how do you focus? What else can you do? What you can do is reach deep inside to find more and new love. Love is the great equalizer. At one end of the love spectrum is happiness and hope. At the other end of the spectrum, for those who can't or won't extend their love, awaits sorrow and guilt.

Below, Tom talks appropriately about how he misses romance with his wife. It is not hard to believe he is still working to renew his relationship with his wife, and working hard to work through his disappointments:

> *Taking care of a spouse is not for the faint hearted. I don't mind the housework, the shopping and the cleaning. My wife can't do those things. I don't mind the labor involved or doing all the cooking. I like to cook. I have a full-time job as well. What I do mind is the total loss of romance, the out for dinner evenings and the pillow talk. They say men are all about sex. That is not true. I miss all the courtship things, the looks, smelling her perfume. All of that is gone. That to me is the most bitter loss. (1)*

Even though this man has disappointments, there are still things he can do to add romance to their lives. I get it that he misses his wife's perfume. But can't he help her use the perfume? Can't he help her put on a special outfit and have a special dinner? Even if she can't go out, can't he have food delivered from a once favorite restaurant they shared? Love does not have to be lost.

Love Can Be Rekindled

IN STEVEN COVEY'S GLOBAL, bestselling book, *7 Habits of Highly Effective People*, he stated that love does not have to be permanently lost. Love can be rekindled if necessary. He gave as his reference the new mother who suffers extreme discomfort and pain during both the pregnancy and the delivery. Yet, she becomes overwhelmed with love when she, for the first time, is able to see and embrace her new-born child. That is somewhat similar to the caregiver's plight. However, contrary to the mother who seems to generate new love for her new born child, caregivers sometimes allow their love for their loved one not to increase, but to decrease, and even disappear.

Caregivers' comments often pointed to the fact they had earlier loved, but that their original love was now gone. They expressed guilt and sorrow but felt there was little they could do about it. I believe there is something that they and you can do about it. They can take Steve Covey's advice and love their way back, through renewed romance, into a giving relationship.

So, What Should Be Done Regarding Romance?

CONTRARY TO WHAT MAY have inspired your earlier yearnings, the care recipients I interviewed currently desired simple contact and communication with their partner--holding hands, moments of intimacy, a trip out for ice cream, going to the movies, going for automobile rides, watching TV together, regular civil communication, running errands on request, sharing common interests, spending time with family members, ability to resolve issues, willingness to discuss the future, in depth discussions about religion and what comes next, being a good listener, financial expenditures, discussing joint and individual responsibilities, dealing with crisis responsibly and how best to spend the time. Most of these items would not have been considered earlier as romantic, but, successfully executed, may very well be thought of romantic now. For most individuals, being able to obtain the attention and action of their caregivers was considered not only considerate, but also romantic. After all, what makes us happy and feels like love, feels like romance.

I urge you to renew your romance once again. Examine what made the love between you grow in the beginning and ask hard questions. Do you still feel love for the patient? What is missing now? Can you recover any of the things which made your love possible? Are your current feelings the same as when your romance was at its peak? Do you long for those same feelings again? Do you wish you could go back when you were the happiest? Or, are you still very much in love, and still feeling affection for the loved one you serve? Do you still want to do for and care for that person? It depends on which side of love you find yourself. For some, love may be growing, or at least maintaining. For others, love may be slowly disappearing. For the latter caregivers, happiness may be evading you. The loss of romance tends to rob you of the happiness you have previously known.

If you do not feel happy now, it is probably because you also don't feel love. If you do not know whether or not you still feel love for the patient, think about what that individual used to mean to you. Are those feelings tender, romantic and kind? Do those feelings stir up old longings? Old love can become new love through romance.

While this short-book is about you and your possible feelings of lost love, it would not be wise to ignore what your loved one is feeling. What they enjoy and want are critical to your caregiving success, and ultimately an improvement in the romance that you feel for him or her.

Rediscover what it means to experience the joy of a meaningful relationship again. You deserve to be happy. You deserve to feel love. The ultimate would be to rekindle a new kind of love, a long-term, romantic love.

Set a date night and keep it! Even if your loved one is unable to go out, still have a date night and do something special for both of you. Love can be rekindled. If it requires a change in attitude and then for you to take action.

FINAL COMMENTS ABOUT ROMANCE

I RECENTLY HEARD FROM a diligent friend who, when his wife had a setback, determined he loved her and would be there for her. He promised her that, "He was all hers, and she would be his major commitment." He knew what he was getting into when he made that enormous time commitment. For eight years he has kept his promise and has kept his romance alive. Every couple relationship will embrace that issue. One person out of each couple will likely realize that responsibility. Now is a good time to tighten up the romance to insure when that day comes, your relationship will withstand the final responsibilities of caregiving and obtain its joys.

6.

THE FORGIVENESS

Forgive others, not because they deserve forgiveness, but because you deserve peace

– Jonathan Lockwood Huie

Can You Accept Your Situation?

THERE IS A PERVASIVE and destructive misconception that life should always be easy, and any difficulties met are a red flag of some sinister plot against you. The journey and the dream are inexplicably bound, one cannot be separated from the other, especially if you are to realize your purpose in life. Growth, real love, and hope come through accepting and embracing the struggles in life as well as the joys. (8)

Accepting your situation does not mean giving up. No, there is too much at stake. So, let's dig deep and let me ask you, do you resent fate, or your loved one, for putting you into a caregiving situation? Do you resent others not helping you as much as you think they should? Are you angry inside? To improve your relationship with your loved one and to realize your full potential, you must forgive fate and your loved one for the circumstances you are in. You must let go of the anger or the resentment to find joy and peace. Love in a relationship depends on your change of attitude and the kindly nature of your service. Your heart and your reactions and your actions are the only things you can change to make your situation better. You cannot change your loved one. But by shifting the dynamics of the relationship through loving service you will lay the fertile ground for your loved one to change, and for you both to find peace and happiness.

Unkind Conduct of Loved One

FAR TOO MANY CAREGIVERS become hurt, angry, and frustrated when faced with the unkind, and sometimes abusive conduct of their loved ones. Ill loved ones, who are mad at the world for their circumstances, can be unthankful, nasty, uncomplimentary, and almost impossible to live with. Dedicated caregivers are torn between the love they feel (or have felt) and the unseemly behavior of the ones they are trying to serve and please. This contrast between their caring service and the abusive behavior of their loved ones is hard to understand, let alone accept.

Your loved one, through kindness, can be helped to find forgiveness in his or her heart for the devastating events in life that has left him or her dependent upon others for every need and survival.

Humans have a natural inclination to respond in kind to the actions of others. So, it is possible your forgiveness of a loved one's unappreciative and angry behavior can change his or her heart and lead him or her to discover love and peace. It is hard to be unkind when continually confronted by kindness and love. But regardless of your patient's behavior, your willingness to forgive your loved one, yourself, and others, enables you to continue with your caregiving responsibilities with a new-found peace and strength.

This wife feels she has lost her love for her difficult husband, but determined to remain positive, she still carries on with her responsibilities and may yet forgive and help him were she to understand the possibilities in the power of forgiveness.

I have been in a difficult marriage for 34 years and my love for him has disappeared, but I still care for the guy. He is handicapped due to weight issues and our health insurance not willing to pay for bariatric surgery or to have a lump removed off his thigh so he can have knee replacements. Therefore, he cannot walk very far and I am constantly waiting on him to get whatever he needs. I have to do it all, carry in the groceries, put his socks and shoes on, put his power chair in and out of the van, pump gas, plus cleaning, laundry, dishes, clean up after him, etc., and go to work every day. I have let my health go and I am now experiencing back pain from the bending and lifting. Most days he is very depressed and I try to keep him positive and me too. My husband does still work every day when he can. But with his walking issues, his working days are just about over. Since he is considered self-employed, when he doesn't work, he doesn't get paid. I don't know what is going to happen to us when that day comes. (1)

He is in denial of the fact that our marriage is not meeting my needs and gets very angry if I try to explain why I am not as enthusiastic about him and that I don't think of him in an intimate way anymore. We haven't been intimate for several years now. He calls me at work to tell me what he needs and to stop at the store and get him this and that, and then when I come home he expects me to be attentive to all his needs and his desire for conversation. He is also not a happy camper when it comes to his situation and is grumpy and irritable most of the day. Then he forgets that he said rude things to me and claims he doesn't remember any of it.

I am not "In Love" with him anymore, but I love him as my long-time husband. I can understand what others are saying about loneliness and being alone. I get so tired and depressed sometimes and he doesn't seem to understand that. When other people come around, he will act all cheerful and happy but the minute they leave, he goes back to his depressed state. He falls asleep when I talk to him and then claims that he is listening. (1).

Forgiving is Healing

WHAT MAY BE MISSING in many lost love relationships, if not all of them, is forgiveness. It is hard to forgive another person who is mistreating you. It is hard to forgive and forget when your heart is aching and your body and mind are fatigued. But, your increased forgiveness can change your own attitude, as well as your loved one's attitude. Forgiveness will enable you to work past the unkind behavior, even if your loved one doesn't change. However, it is likely there will be a change for the better. Forgiveness is hope.

Work on Your Attitude Every Day

DON'T EXPECT TO BECOME all forgiving and more hopeful in a day. You can't simply turn on or off a switch to your feelings and habits.

Becoming forgiving and hopeful requires you to work on your attitude every day. It is a goal you set for your life and your relationships. Take this process one day at a time, and focus your attention on the aspects of your life that you have control over. (8) Your hope and self-confidence will multiply as your love and your ability to forgive grows. I believe it is good to remember what Mahatma Ghandi said, "The weak can never forgive. Forgiveness is the attribute of the strong." I believe forgiveness really is a sign of strength!

Be Forgiving In Challenging Situations

FUNCTIONING WITH FORGIVENESS AND hope in situations that cause distress, and derail motivation, must be learned. As a caregiver, you must do research into the specifics of your situation, your loved one's condition, and the related emotional impact of becoming a caregiver. Arm yourself with knowledge and understanding, so you can be comfortable in the tasks you will face. Studies show that learning to be more comfortable in threatening situations can actually reduce the risk for physical health problems and improve overall psychological functioning. (8)

Support groups, or a supportive friend who can talk over your situation and help you find a foundation of forgiveness and love in a difficult situation, are important. Remember, you are not alone in your situation. There are many caregivers struggling with the burdens of providing for a loved one, and need your support as well. Ask for and find help. Do not shoulder your burdens alone. I know it seems unbelievable, but many people either don't think to offer to help or are afraid to help because they fear the responsibilities of being a care provider. You take the initiative to ask for the help you need and help that person to be comfortable with being an interim caregiver. Helping each other can arm you both with an abundance of hope and forgiveness and greatly reduce stress for everyone. Health, joy, peace, and love should not be lost in the caregiving situation and won't be if you set the right goals and work every day in the right direction. Forgiveness and hope are love's constant companions.

Challenge Your Negative Thoughts
<u>Rather Than Dwell on Them</u>

NEGATIVE THOUGHTS WILL UNDERMINE everything you try to achieve and rob you of the true rewards of forgiveness and hope. Only you can deal with your negative thoughts and stop letting them control your life and your future. First, caregivers must engage with their difficult emotions when they arise. You can't ignore them. You need to examine them and determine why you are having those feelings. What is causing them? Is it something inside you? Is it something your loved one is doing? Understanding the situation is the first step in dealing with emotions in a constructive manner. This allows you to have control over the emotions, rather than letting them rule you. Once you know what you are facing and why you are feeling the way you are, then you can find solutions for the problem and choose to develop positive thoughts about the problem. The fear and worry you suppressed or dwelt on will fade. Your positive thoughts will allow forgiveness to blossom and love to grow.

Forgiveness Enables Love to Grow

SOME CAREGIVERS SAY THEIR service actually drew them closer to the person being served. They say deep friendships had been formed and they speak with fondness about their experiences. This is completely opposite from what other caregivers report and what we covered previously. For these caregivers, the responsibility did not chase away their love for their loved one. How? Is it possible? What about in situations with an unappreciative patient? Are there ways to avoid the tragedy of diminishing love? Service should not depreciate love. Service, combined with forgiveness, should magnify it.

After You've Tried All Else – Try Love

HAVE YOU TRIED EVERYTHING you can think of to help your loved one and nothing has worked? Are you at your wits end and have no hope? I know it sounds pat, and just too simple, but love is the key that unlocks the heart. And the heart is truly what drives every person's life and ability to overcome difficulty.

Love is the answer. So, anything you can do to increase the love in your situation is the right choice to make. While love should be the first step and not a last resort, it needs to be put into action. What is love in action? Love is patient, kind, not jealous, angry, or self-serving, Love protects, hopes, trusts, and preserves. So many lives have been changed by love and the actions that go with it – forgiving, touching, speaking, feeling, smiling, inspiring, etc. It is never too late to try.

Listen to the story of someone who did try:

Relationship restored! Here is my story to the world on how I got my love back and saved my marriage. I really love James so much that I cannot even do without him. I was married for seven years with two kids and we lived happily until things started getting ugly and we had a fight and argument almost every time . . . it got worse at a point that he filed for divorce . . . I tried my best to make him change his mind and stay with me because I love him with all my heart and didn't want to lose him but everything just proved abortive . . . He moved out of the house and still went ahead to file for divorce . . . I pleaded, cried and tried everything but still nothing worked. The breakthrough came when someone introduced me to this wonderful man who eventually helped me out . . . Within two days James called me and was sorry for the emotional trauma he had cost me, moved back to the house and we continue to live happily, the kids are happy too and we are expecting our third child. I have introduced my friend to a lot of couples with problems across the world and they have had good news . . . Just thought I should spread my experience because I strongly believe someone out there needs it. Don't give up just yet, the difference between 'Ordinary' & 'Extra-ordinary' is the 'Extra' so make extra effort to save your marriage/relationship if it's truly worth it. (1)

Love Can Win Out in the End

THERE ARE TIMES WHEN, regardless of what you do, no matter how hard you try, an end comes. Death is every bit as much of life's story as life itself. But, the end does not always have to have a bitter taste.

Discover how Janet learned to understand the most critical issues of love and forgiveness and how beautifully she describes the end of her expanded service:

> *My husband ... had MS since diagnosis in 2002, walked with a cane for 8 years, then started losing his balance, falling, and also losing his mental faculties through Dementia and Macular Degeneration. He had been exposed to Agent Orange in Vietnam and developed Parkinson's as well. His son Michael helped a great deal by paying for caregivers so I was not alone in this task. We also had the aid of Hospice, early on! I loved this man dearly and was able to share in movies and concerts with him, even in our Senior Club although his participation was quite limited.*
>
> *The caregiving was very difficult for me, but I did acquire some nursing skills, after he needed help from April of 2010 until his death in October of 2011. So, my caregiving lasted for about a year and a half. We had no family or relatives nearby and that was the hardest of all. Michael, my stepson was a busy lawyer who lived 75 miles away ... but bless his heart, he came to help as often as possible, probably about twice a month.*
>
> *You just have to "hang in" there and be a spouse to your spouse through all the trials, but only with the help of our Almighty Father in Heaven. He gave me the strength and courage to carry on. Now my husband is at peace with the Lord, which he certainly earned as he was the most, generous and kindest man I have ever known. (1)*

The responsibilities of caregiving duties are difficult when being mistreated or unappreciated by the one receiving the care. Even when conditions are positive, the burden of caregiving can be hard to bear.

One way to develop a better attitude and ease the responsibility of caring for your patient and others, is to make a list of key responsibilities you will always take care of, and determine which of those duties are causing relationship problems. Discuss this with your patient or your support system. See what help can be gained with those chores, then focus on finding forgiveness in your heart for the burdens you bear.

FINAL COMMENTS ABOUT FORGIVENESS

Robert Muller said, "To forgive is the highest, most beautiful form of love. In return, you will receive untold peace and happiness." The loneliness and fatigue experienced by the caretaker, places the caretaker in a vulnerable, emotional state. Tired and frustrated, the negative conduct of a loved one takes its toll and love slips away. Attitude and commitment must be addressed to gain hope and love. A new relationship can be formed. Love and forgiveness can outweigh negative emotions and overcome difficult situations. Forgiveness makes it possible for love to exist and love is the only lasting way for the relationship to survive. Love, joy, and happiness can be found, but it is up to you to make it happen.

7.

THE DIVORCE

When you loved someone and you had to let her go, there will always be that small part that whispers, "what was it that you wanted and why didn't you fight for it?
– Shannon L. Alder

―――――― ♪ ――――――

Divorce Is Not Without Grief

DIVORCE IS THE DEATH of a marriage (3). I have watched and counseled many considering divorce. For most of them who eventually did divorce, it was not a solution. It fact, it was the reverse. Most divorces bring sorrow, sadness, regret, grief, and frustration. Children are negatively impacted, and lives irreparably damaged. The questions must be asked: Where would you go? Where would you live? Who can you trust? Is a second marriage the solution? How can you know it will be better? Will that love last? Are you assured happiness? Can you again find love?

Love can be blind to reality and so can divorce. Don't let the influences of fatigue and loneliness influence you to believe that divorce is the solution. Living with divorce may be more difficult than living with your current loved one.

Heather is struggling with the thought of divorce. Her story is a sad one, and it is easy to feel sympathy for her situation:

> *I very much know these feelings. You said something that resounded. It's different being with your sweetheart than it is being a caregiver. That is true. It totally changes the relationship. For me, I've struggled with the thought of divorce or separation because I feel that this is not "married" but something else. I go through tremendous loneliness.*
>
> *I believe that God sees my situation and has plans to change it in due season. But for now, I stay. I've often asked myself what is the true reason why I stay. I always come back to LOVE. It is the reason. Love, honor and commitment are what keep me going. I love my husband and have battled this disease with him since I was 26! I get really mad when I see articles talking about caregivers and it's always older people in their 50s plus. I know very few people in their 20s that take care of disabled spouses. Most of them would have bailed out early. I didn't. I've stayed through it all, and now I'm 39. Everywhere I go I am told I am a beautiful woman, but I am in a sexless marriage and haven't been touched in years. Most people don't know this. It is emotionally and mentally straining. For now, I just soldier on and believe that one day things will change. (1)*

Remember How Good It Was

IF I WERE TO attempt to remember what has been good in my marriage, I would remember saying "I love you" every day and meaning it. I would remember how I felt the first time I saw Wendy. I would remember how many wonderful things we enjoyed while dating. I would remember the excitement I experienced upon meeting her family. I would remember the thrill of selecting her engagement ring. I would remember all that was associated with getting married, and I would remember the joy of our marriage. I would remember selecting the furniture for our first apartment. I would remember the pride we shared as I was professionally promoted. I would remember how well we were able to resolve difficult issues.

I would remember the birth of our first child, a daughter, Holly. I would remember the sorrow of losing our second child, another daughter. I would remember the excitement of the next four births, all sons. I would remember the transfers to other cities and the promotions that prompted those transfers. I would remember all of our 14 homes and the wonderful friends we knew. I would remember volunteer service and how we shared those moments. I wouldn't remember the sorrows and disappointments, but I might remember the wonder of overcoming those obstacles. I remember how lively and quick-minded Wendy was during emergencies, and there were many. I would remember all those years of living with her, and loving her, and appreciating her. I would remember how good and generous she was. I would remember her support and loyalty to me and our children.

You see, I remember only the good things, although there must have been some bad, my memory fails because my focus is on the positive. I want it to be there. I just want to remember everything about our relationship with joy and fondness. Can that be called love? I hope so. I want to remember it all with love. What will you remember? It is never too late to increase your love by remembering. There is an ever-increasing supply of love available, if you look for it.

Reasons For Divorce

AMONG THE MOST COMMON 'reasons' people give for their divorces are lack of commitment, too much arguing, infidelity, marrying too young, unrealistic expectations, lack of equality in the relationship, lack of preparation for marriage, abuse and failing to agree on how money should be spent. Some of these problems can be fixed, and divorce prevented. Some cannot.

Just keep in mind that divorce may conclude one set of problems, but another set of problems always waits nearby. Caregivers are advised to tread carefully regarding divorce. Although the caregiving duties may be heavy and the pressures intense, the alternative might be worse.

This frustrated woman is considering divorce, but is conflicted because she knows she has responsibility for her husband as well as for the marriage:

My first husband died at age 34, when I was just 30. I had been with him since my late teens. I unexpectedly remarried one of our friends several years later, and we had two girls. He has had addiction issues, mental health issues, and severe health issues. I am a registered nurse, so I act like his nurse, and not his wife. I get paid to be nurse, I never asked for my husband to be my patient, too. I feel guilty because I want a divorce or an affair sometimes. My wedding vows haunt me. I have been faithful, but don't know how much longer I can be/feel so alone. (1)

Reasons Partners Should Stay Together

THERE ARE MANY COUPLES breaking up today. It is easy! But simplicity is not a virtue in this instance. Commitment should mean something. Below are reasons known relationship experts have advanced as to why couples should stay married. Most good marriages will include many of these reasons:

Half of The People in Your Current Marriage Will Be in Your Next Relationship

YEP, THAT'S RIGHT. SOME of the problems in your current marriage have to do with you. So, prematurely running away from a current marriage "may" simply result in transporting those same issues to your next relationship. Better to resolve them in the current marriage and grow as a result. Reconsider your divorce thoughts – caregiving is better.

Re-Entering the World Of Dating

DO YOU REALLY WANT to begin the process of finding someone to trust, love and respect starting from scratch? If you've watched any of the popular reality shows, you know the world is full of people who have, shall we say, relationship development issues. The grass is rarely greener on the other side.

The Kids

I KNOW IT'S NOT in vogue to admit many people are still married because of the kids, but it's a reality. Once children enter the picture, every decision you make impacts the entire family not just the two of you. Therefore, it's okay if your joint desire to care for the kids keeps you together during some rough patches. To be clear, I'm *not* saying this is the only reason to stay in a marriage, but it is a massively important reason to remain in the game and continue caregiving.

The Person You Married Is Still There

I DON'T BELIEVE PEOPLE get married so they can get divorced. That would be dumb. Let's face it, we all take our spouses for granted from time to time. Try this, make a list of all of the positive attributes that led you to marry your spouse. If most attributes still exist, there is still hope for the relationship. (5)

In Katie's story, she is striving to be positive and influence her husband:

> *Hello, I am becoming a caregiver to my sweet wonderful husband he is 59, I am 52. He was recently diagnosed with ALS. We are both on our second marriage and never knew it could be as wonderful as it has been. Now, I am working full time as well as the fulltime cook, parent, house keeper and all. I lay in bed wondering how to pay the bills, meet the needs of my husband and those of our teenager and still remember myself. We have talked that things are not the same as they were. It is sad, but as I live each day to touch him, look into his beautiful eyes and know our*

days are literally numbered, I treasure those little smiles and touches. Wishing you all the best, and sending you all strength. (1)

If you are considering divorce, give some serious time thinking about why. What are the "grounds" (legal reasons) for your decision? Are there other solutions to resolve your problems? Have you truly exhausted all other options? Have you tried with all of your heart to repair your relationship? As I said divorce is a seemingly easy answer these days, but rarely the right one. Once it is done, an entirely new world of problems unfolds. Caregivers, even though frustrated, should be slow to choose divorce as a solution to their situations. Before considering this step, a partner must first get a clear picture of his once loved one and develop a better attitude about her and the situation. What are the reasons you have to stay together? Be honest and be complete. Why did you marry this person? Do any of those reason reasons still exist? Have you truly given your all to be your partner's best friend, lover, and confidant? Or can you only see your unhappiness, your frustrations, your feelings, and your disappointments? Don't let easy rob you from growing and discovering what real love is all about.

FINAL COMMENTS ABOUT DIVORCE

A study of baby boomers caring for aging parents by *The Caring. com* uncovered the following:

- 80% of baby boomers reported caregiving strained their relationships.
- 46% of baby boomers stated that caregiving damaged their romantic relationships.

- 25% of divorced baby boomers said caregiving played a major role in their divorce.

It is clearly obvious that caregiving impacts a marriage relationship, even some ending in divorce. Learning these facts in advance can help caregivers avoid the mistakes others have made. Don't let the caregiving responsibilities rob you of a potentially, wonderful future relationship.

8.

THE EXPECTATIONS

Don't lower your expectations to meet your performance. Raise your level of performance to meet your expectations.

– Ralph Marston

Real Love Can Motivate Everyone

THOSE WHO SERVE OTHERS grow to love them. Those who receive that service grow to love those who serve them. We should not expect anything to the contrary. Except in many of the caregiving examples, love seems to be lost because of the service. Is it possible that serving is not why the love is lost? Why doesn't love increase in those situations involving caregivers? Is it the length, or the severity of the service? Is it the enormity of the physical tasks? Is it because a caregiver's expectations in relationships and life don't match up to the reality now being faced ? Is it possible a new kind of love needs to be extended by the caregiver? What would happen if a dependent loved one truly felt this

new love from her caregiver? Would the patient be amazed and motivated to return that love in her responses?

Disappointed Expectations Can Feel Like a <u>Loss of Love</u>

IT IS NATURAL TO set goals and objectives in life. We are intended to
climb and reach for wanted expectations. In business, young executives
are taught there are two budgetary goals, the first is what is expected
and needed to perpetuate the business, and the reach goal which is
beyond the first goal and thought to be attainable only if commitment
and effort are generously extended. Likening that to caregiving, it is
reasonable to expect certain conduct and actions will produce a projected response for the service, treatment and love you provide for your
patient? Should that include a reach goal such as in business? Maybe
not, but you get the idea—going above and beyond the expected can
generate greater results.

But what if the needed expectations are not met? More specifically,
what if your expectations of your loved one or your own feelings of love
for that person are disappointing. Should the disappointment or realization of the missed goal lessen your affection for the patient, someone
for whom you care? Your disappointment might feel like a loss of love,
but is it? Should their unwillingness or lack of concern drive a change
in your attitude? I think the answer to each question is no. Love is not
like a trophy or coveted award for which there is only victory or loss.
Love is not a commodity up for temporary gain or loss. It's a muscle
which becomes stronger and healthier with exercise. A muscle requiring
preparation for any difficult task. An athlete trains for a marathon. He
doesn't win the race or even reach the finish line without planning and

training his body. Such is love. It's a reachable goal which should be sought for, planned for and developed over time.

Below, Katie tried it. She has the right attitude, but still is stressed:

> . . . *I've been searching for years to find help for spouses who care for their spouses but never could find any. I married my husband 10 years ago and knew he had some serious health issues including a heart condition and circulation issues. No one could have ever prepared me for what was in store. I love him dearly and we have an amazing relationship centered around Christ but there are times I just don't know what to do with myself. I struggle with having sympathy as I'm a person constantly on the move. He doesn't hold me back and encourages me to continue doing fun things. We now have three kids and I struggle balancing teaching fulltime, being a mom fulltime and a wife fulltime. It helps when he says how appreciative he is of me, but sometimes it's just not enough. He's on disability and works part time, but when he's sick of course he loses out on that pay. Thankfully, God fills in the gaps but it is quite a challenge. It is very hard for me to allow others to help me. I feel like a poor, charity case that can't take care of her family . . . (1)*

Expectations and Disappointments

ROMANCE IS LIKE A trained pigeon, regardless of how far it flies, it should always return to you. However, I have owned pigeons; sometimes they don't return. Their failure to return was always a disappointment. But, I didn't give up on those that remained. I have been a sports fan and participant all my life. Sometimes my team of choice, or my personal efforts, ended in disappointment. But neither the pigeons, nor the sports participants give up when the "trip" is difficult. Our lives today have no provision for disappointing results. We are taught early on to gloss over disappointment rather than face it. Every kid today gets an award just so they don't have to be disappointed. We do ourselves a disservice by not realizing how much a part of life disappointment is.

Disappointments must be experienced and absorbed. They can be a mentor in our lives from which we learn to grow and develop resilience. We can reflect on our disappointments, on what we did wrong, or what went wrong and try harder in the future. All relationships come with disappointments and how we deal with them determines what kind of relationship we build. Marital and personal relationships are the most dynamic relationships in our lives, full of joys and disappointments. When faced with disappointed expectations, what response will eventually lead to the ultimate goal of love and happiness? Going beyond the expected? Extending loving kindness, concern, and hope for the future despite your own disappointment? Or turning away from your partner and letting resentment, anger, and depression fill your heart? I have experienced disappointment in my relationship with my wife. I know these feelings. I have not always been right in my response to my disappointments. But when I did reach beyond and act with loving kindness, the relationship blossomed and our love became stronger. Only then were my expectations finally fulfilled.

<u>Real Love Should Never Be a Surprise</u>

REAL LOVE MUST BE intentionally cultivated. While there are many 'love at first sight" stories, they are not usually founded upon real love. Loving another person is not like loving a good movie or a great book.

So many mistakes have been made in the name of spontaneous love. That is why it is unfortunate anyone would abandon their loved one of many years because the going gets rough. The 'till death do us part' nomenclature is for real. It is not just set in legal language but it is a moral and personal obligation. Surprises are for carnivals and circuses. The human endeavor is far more critical.

Love is more than an understood and prepared emotion, it is an action we take no matter how we "feel." This is what makes the commitment of love stable. It enables human beings to go beyond normal efforts because they aren't making their decisions based on feelings, but on purpose. Love in action self-perpetuates. By making the right choices and developing the right responses, it spurs on human efforts and advances a loving relationship to greater heights. Caregivers who are concerned about losing their love should take heart. If your love feels lost, or if your love is slipping, don't be discouraged – but do something about it. For some, it may not be easy. For others, it will be exhilarating. If you expand your efforts, you have a right to expect your love to grow. Love should not be a surprise. Love should be purposeful, uplifting, and lovely.

Below are comments about a man who has addressed his difficulties head on. He is realistic, yet hopeful. He is willing to "power up and handle it". With his attitude, he will handle it – well!

My wife, 52, is working on battling her third brain tumor in seven and one-half years. They – the doctors told us there wasn't much hope several years ago, but she has defied the statistics and continues to work and live as normally as possible. She also had a brain bleed but recovered, and has had two major brain tumor removal surgeries. I understand there is hope. There is also a place called Well Spouse Association that may be a resource for you. I just found it for myself. As men, we sometimes think we can tough it out and power up and "handle it" – but I've found that whenever a spouse is ill or injured, there are two people who need help – both spouses need care, support and understanding from others who can relate and have experienced similar challenges. (1)

What Do You Want to Receive?

TENDER MOMENTS COME TO all ages, all genders and others who deserve it and sometimes to even those who don't. Tender moments begin with caring, then with sharing, and then with daring. In the beginning, you probably dared to seek real love by making commitments and risking your future with someone you loved. Similar conditions exist now. There can still be caring and sharing, but the daring is different. Might you still want those same emotions if it were possible? Might you still want the happiness and joy awarded to those who make the effort and commitment?

So, ask yourself what you want to receive from your caregiving experience. What relationship do you want to have with your loved one? Be realistic in your expectations and the amount of change you want your loved one to make. Be patient. Realize change is never easy and takes time. Then be positive, believe in that change, and respond with loving kindness that reaches beyond what is needed to maintain the norm. Set your reach goal to be one of joy and happiness with your loved one. And most importantly, enjoy the journey. Realize the path to change can be as enjoyable as reaching your goal and celebrate every step along the way.

Here a woman feels her life is difficult, and yet is willing to keep working at supporting her husband, all the while carrying the burdens she has been given:

> I am 39 and my husband has had kidney disease almost our entire marriage. He had a transplant (my kidney) but it failed last year and now I do his dialysis at home. He is a good loving man but this trial has been so long and a lonely road for each of us since we are in a different stage of our relationship. Being a caregiver totally changes everything. It's not like being with your sweetheart. . . . It's true. As for the feeling of fear that things will only linger on and you will be stuck in this the rest of your life, those fears are all too familiar for me also. I see it sometimes as living in the "gray area" where there is neither full life or an end. I've struggled often with feeling of simply wanting a new life to the point I've even thought of separation, but then God comforts me and encourages me to love to the end. It's what keeps me here.
>
> . . . I feel like I am being tried in the refining fire of true love and yes, it is so, so hard! I've said that same exact thing to my best friend. Some days you just want it to end and start life afresh. I've struggled with guilty feeling for that myself, but God understands these feelings. He knows how heavy the yoke is that I carry! I really believe that my reward will come . . . if I will just press forward. (1)

What Are You Willing to Give?

EVERYONE WILL HAVE A different list of those things that will bring happiness and serenity to their lives. I suspect an increase of love will be on every list, but in different priority. Do you know what will make you happy? Do you know what will make your loved one happy? Do you know what you require of your loved one? Do you know what you require of yourself? Are you willing to try as hard as you expect your loved one to try? Are you willing to try even if the expected term of life is short? Do you still want to make that person happy? Do you ache for the aches of your loved one? Do you want the assurances of really being loved in your life again? Do you ache for someone to love you – really love you? The answers to those questions will likely point you in the right direction.

How Do I See Her Now?

IF I TOOK A test today about my true love, and had to respond in an essay, I would welcome a chance. I would honestly say, "I love her now as much as any time in our lives. Though physically it is not the same, emotionally it is stronger. She is still interesting. We don't always agree, but we share honestly, and have common interests and activities we do together. She is supportive, attentive, generous, kind, sensitive, responsive, energetic, intelligent, loyal and, most important, loving. She makes my life better. She magnifies my possibilities. She challenges me to do better. She cares about things that are important to me, which makes it easy for me to care about what is important to her. She provides tender moments for me. I have hope for our future and joy in our present. I like that! She makes me feel loved.

Expectations in life are normal. But don't base them by comparing yourself to other people around you. Others always seem to have it all. They appear to have few, if any, problems. That is not the case, because everyone has his or her own set of difficulties in life. So, to develop a better attitude regarding the expectations of your life, you need to examine the source of your expectations. Have your expectations been placed upon you by someone else? Are they realistic or unrealistic for your injured or ill loved one? Are your expectations born out of envy, or a true desire within your own heart? Consider what your expectations of your loved one are making your loved one feel. What would your life together be like if those expectations were greater than what you thought were achievable? Or, what would it be like if there were no expectations placed upon you?

FINAL COMMENTS ABOUT EXPECTATIONS

I heard a definition for expectations: *"the hope, confidence and assumption that something good is going to happen in the future."* That good should be a strengthening of your love for your patient - and your commitment. Because, regardless of whatever the person may have done to discourage you, or deflate your affection, your expectations will hold steady. It is a commitment that you will be there when needed, and will make life better because *you* will be better. Be a believer. Believe you can make the difference in your loved one's life, which will in turn make a difference in yours. Your expectations for a re-kindling of love can be realized by your determination to meet both of your positive expectations.

9.

THE ULTIMATE TEST

The only love worthy of a name is unconditional.
– John Powell

———————— ⸙ ————————

LOVE IS A SPECIAL and complicated emotion which is quite difficult to understand. Although most people believe that love revolves around the heart, it actually occurs in the brain, which sends messages to the heart. There are many definitions or types of love. Most of them have a reference back to ancient Greece. The following are the most frequently used Greek definitions:

Eros, or Sexual Passion

THE FIRST KIND OF love was Eros, named after the Greek god of fertility, and it represented the idea of sexual passion and desire. But the Greeks didn't always think of it as something positive, as we tend to do today. In fact, Eros was viewed as a dangerous, fiery, and irrational form of love that could take hold of you and possess you—an attitude shared by many later spiritual thinkers.

Eros is a passionate and intense love that arouses romantic feelings; it is the kind that often triggers "high" feelings in a new relationship and makes you say, "I love him/her." It is simply an emotional and sexual love. Although this romantic love is important in the beginning of a new relationship, it may not last unless it moves a notch higher because the focus is more on one's own feelings instead of the other person's. If people "in love" do not feel good about their relationship anymore, they will stop loving their partner.

Philia, or Deep Friendship

THE SECOND VARIETY OF love was Philia, affectionate love or friendship, which the Greeks valued far more than the base sexuality of Eros. Philia concerned the deep comradery friendship that developed between brothers in arms who had fought side by side on the battlefield. It was about showing loyalty to your friends, sacrificing for them, as well as sharing your emotions with them.

Ludus, or Playful Love

THIS WAS THE GREEKS' idea of playful love, which referred to the affection between children or young lovers. We've all had a taste of it in the flirting and teasing in the early stages of a relationship. But we also live out our Ludus when we sit around in a bar bantering and laughing with friends, or when we go out dancing.

STORGE, or Familiar Love

IT IS A KIND of family, familiar, or friendship love. This is the love that parents naturally feel for their children; the love that members of the family have for each other; or the love that friends feel for each other. In some cases, this friendship love may turn into a romantic relationship, and the couple in such a relationship become best friends. Storge love is unconditional, accepts flaws or faults and ultimately drives you to forgive. It's committed, sacrificial and makes you feel secure, comfortable and safe.

PHILEO, Warm or Tender Platonic Love

THE PHILEO LOVE REFERS to an affectionate, warm and tender platonic love. It makes you desire friendship with someone. It's the kind of love which livens up the Agape (defined at end of list) love. Although you may have an Agape love for your enemies, you may not have a Phileo love for the same people. The translation of the word Phileo is love in the noun – form: it is how you feel about someone. It is a committed and chosen love.

Philautia, or Love of the Self

THE GREEK'S NEXT CATEGORY of love was Philautiasr self-love. And the clever Greeks realized there were two types. One was an unhealthy variety associated with narcissism, where you became self-obsessed and focused on personal fame and fortune. A healthier version enhanced your wider capacity to love.

The idea was that if you like yourself and feel secure in yourself, you will have plenty of love to give others (as is reflected in the Buddhist-inspired concept of "self-compassion"). Or, as Aristotle put it, *All friendly feelings for others are an extension of a man's feelings for himself.*

Pragma, and Enduring, or Longstanding Love

Another Greek love was the mature love known as Pragma. This was the deep understanding that developed between long-married couples. Pragma is about making compromises to help the relationship work over time, and showing patience and tolerance.

The psychoanalyst Erich Fromm said that we expend too much energy on "falling in love" and need to learn more how to "stand in love." Pragma is precisely about standing in love—making an effort to give love rather than just receive it.

Agape, or Selfless Love, or Love for Everyone

The final category of love, and perhaps the most radical, is agape or selfless love. This is a love that you extend to all people, whether family members or distant strangers. C.S. Lewis referred to it as "gift love," the highest form of Christian love. It is the name of our love for God. There is growing evidence that Agape is in a dangerous decline in many countries. Empathy levels in the U.S. have dropped sharply over the past 40 years, with the steepest fall occurring in the past decade.

Agape is an unconditional love that sees beyond the outer surface and accepts the recipient for whom he/she is, regardless of his/her flaws, shortcomings or faults. It's the type of love that everyone strives to have for his fellow human beings. Although you may not like someone, you decide to love him just as a human being. This kind of love is all about sacrifice as well as giving and expecting nothing in return. The translation of the word agape is love in the verb form: it is the love demonstrated by your behavior towards another person. It is a committed and chosen love. (20)

By combining Pragma and Agape love in a relationship, we can say that unconditional love means loving another in his or her essence, as he or she is, no matter what he or she does or fails to do despite the length of the journey. People with ill loved ones should understand this notion best of all. Taking wise instruction from Pragma above, we should be found, "standing in love—making an effort to give love rather than being focused on receiving it." This is done by always asking yourself, "What is the most loving thing I can do for my loved one in this particular moment?"

Love isn't one size fits all; what might be a loving act toward one person could be harmful to another person, because it doesn't help one get closer to being loved and having happiness. Pragma love and Agape love is about making compromises over time for the relationship to work, and showing patience and tolerance. Making daily choices to tenderly and affectionately extend your love will bless both of you. (4)

One must consider your perspective as well. The caregiving situation provides a new kind of closeness that can bring a deeper, richer happiness for you both. A happiness based on kind consideration, expressed affection, and tender and loving responses. Life is about the choices we make when challenges and tests come our way. We can all make a choice to give a kinder, more compassionate, unconditional love.

God's Unconditional Love for Us

THE BIBLE TELLS US "God is love." He is the perfect embodiment of love, and we rely heavily on the constancy and universal reach of that love. President Thomas S. Monson expressed: "God's love is there for you whether or not you feel you deserve love. It is simply always there." (18)

Elder D. Todd Christofferson said the following:

> *There are many ways to describe and speak of divine love. One of the terms we hear often today is that God's love is "1" unconditional." His love is described in scripture as "2" great and wonderful love, "3" perfect love, "4" redeeming love, "5" and "everlasting love." God's love is not conditional on anything we do. His love is unconditional. God's love is infinite and it will endure forever, but what it means for each of us depends on how we respond to His love.* (18)

To believe in unconditional love, and to actually love unconditionally, requires a great deal of thought, action and faith. Only you can decide if and how you can (or should) love unconditionally but, to help, here are my thoughts about loving unconditionally.

The Test of Unconditional Love

WHETHER I LIKE IT or not, life has been a series of tests for me. Not tests with passing or failing grades, but tests, when the right answers are finally found, moves me further along the road of life's journey, maturing me and enriching my life and Wendy's life in every step I make.

These tests are never easy, and for some, can be overwhelming for a season. Note, I said "for a season," because with persistence and belief, perspective, growth, and success are possible.

Developing the capacity to love unconditionally is the ultimate test-filled journey. Many of the tests found on this path, are introduced to us through our family and marriage relationships and tear deeply at our heart strings when things don't go well. For most people, their eventual, deep and lasting love started in the exciting romance of their younger years. As those affectionate feelings expanded over time, a new kind of love emerged—unconditional love. A love where nothing in life can separate your partnership. Your commitment to each other cannot be altered by any of life's unpleasant circumstances. No marriage, or other loving relationship escapes the difficult and trying moments or fluctuating emotions, but those whose total commitment becomes unconditional, will make it through.

Caregiving is a vivid example of an extreme test on the journey of unconditional love that often doesn't go well. Why does this happen? While life-altering, this challenge should not be love-altering or life-threatening. Yet, it often tragically ends with a loss of love, or stress so severe that a caregiver's life is jeopardized. The care of loved ones should not burden our commitment, diminish the romance, or reduce the kind and tender feelings in those relationships. In fact, it should magnify love to greater heights - to become unconditional.

How can a person make this happen?

First, Unconditional Love Starts With a Desire for a Willing Heart

LOVE SHOULD BE FREELY given with a willing heart with no expectation of reward, except possibly for love returned.

While facing the hardships of her world, and dealing with new feelings about physical love, this woman is willing, and committed to achieving her own form of unconditional love:

> *I love my husband more than I can express. It's so hard to watch who he is fades away. Like so many others, I don't mind working and running our home on my own. But work, pharmacy trips, doctor appointments, grocery shopping, and trying to spend quality time with both him and our daughter is exhausting. I read and hear all the advice about taking time for myself, but it's hard to put into practice.*
>
> *For a while I really missed the romance of our relationship. Now, I don't even feel attracted that way anymore. I still love him deeply, and am committed to him wholly, but it feels like a part of us has died. He can still care for himself on a basic level, like showering and getting snacks for himself, and I'm grateful for that. What I miss the most is just being able to talk about everything. Conversations are difficult. It's like he's in another world. I miss him so much, yet he's right here. I rely on my faith in God, and a bigger picture than just this moment. I have a wonderful support system in family and friends. I still feel so alone so often. Reading posts about others in a similar situation both gives me strength, and yet breaks my heart. (1)*

No matter what your circumstances are, committing to love or renew your love to another person is the first step toward unconditional love. As you search for emotional stability and affection, your commitment and willing heart provide the fertile ground for the seeds of unconditional love to take root.

As "love regardless of the conditions" grows, it evolves into a more dynamic, more compelling, and more demandingly giving love. Joy in giving supersedes failed expectations. Being human means, we'll always want our own needs and desires to be fulfilled by someone we love, and that does not happen one-hundred percent of the time. Sometimes in certain situations, it doesn't happen at all. But when the joy of giving, loving, and serving another become more important than anything else, then it happens. When you put the needs of your partner above your own needs, the relationship becomes "something more." Wonderful things can happen.

A parent's love for a child often, instantly becomes unconditional the first time a parent - holds the helpless baby in the parent's arms. A bond forms in which the parent will give everything and do anything for the safety and wellbeing of the child no matter how difficult the circumstances. However, contrary to parents' expanding love for their new-born child, a caregiver's love shrinks rather than increases. Why? What is the difference? Is it because parents willingly commit to loving the child with their whole hearts, and some caregivers don't make that commitment? I am talking about a commitment to love, understand, and help a child, not just do for a child. There is a difference.

Caregivers who have tragically related their loss of love for their loved ones said they had love in the beginning. They express guilt and sorrow for their lost love, but felt there is little they can do about it. I'm here to say something can be done about it. A person can love his or her way back into a lasting relationship by making not just a commitment to do for another person, but to love and understand him or her as well. To find joy in the giving to and helping a loved one is its own reward. Will it be easy? No. Is it possible? Yes.

Unconditional love is an essential part of mature romantic love. This partnership founded on feelings, actions, and expectations can evolve to more satisfying and joyful heights if giving love is determined to be the most important thing. Emphasizing positives, instantly forgiving perceived wrongs rather than searching for them, by seeking tender moments, discovering what touches your partner's heart, and returning his or her affections to you won't be easy. It requires hard work to overcoming obstacles that keep you from loving another person. And believe me, caregiving can be a very big obstacle. But, I know unconditional love will bring great joy to both of you. Keep in mind that no matter how hard loving becomes, not feeling love and or being unable to give love when you yearn to do so, is much harder.

Here a woman offers advice to another woman and brings some clarity to the dynamic subject of unconditional love:

> *Let love be the reason you love your husband. Love is what you want back, and you can have that back, but you must sincerely recreate that love you once had! It is not the love you are afraid of, it's the fear of losing it all over again. If you love him like you did before, the fear of having to go through it again seems unbearable, and it is difficult. But it comes down to what do you want in this life, your husband, or your freedom? There is no guarantee you couldn't go through this type of situation with someone else, and if that happens, what then? I am pro marriage, and doing what the vows placed within you, request when it was made . . . just think*

of what is promised in this life, and what is not. What is the right thing to do!? This will probably come with few options, and probably more sacrifice, but anything worth having is worth fighting for, and I know firsthand how a struggle demands strong people. Life is not always fair, but it is always yours, right? (1)

Second, Believe Unconditional <u>Love Can Be Shaped</u>

If love can be rekindled, and it can be, then the reshaping of love should be with true and important goals in mind. Love is an eternal force. Love is essential. Love leads to happiness. In many cases, nothing is more important than love in caregiving situations. Talidari said, "Unconditional Love is not the case of being blinded by love, but rather the resolution that nothing is more important than love."

There is a higher degree of love to pursue. Unconditional love is that highest degree. Loving unconditionally means it is impossible not to feel love, and demonstrate such for another individual. In fact, when someone loves unconditionally, that person responds in love regardless of the damaging conduct of another. How is that possible? Through goals and purpose set after having a clear picture of what unconditional love is.

Thirdly, Unconditional Love <u>Should be Given Freely</u>

IF YOU HAVE TO do something, or be a certain way, in order to receive love, that love is conditional. If it is given to you freely and without reservation, it is unconditional. Caregivers who volunteer to give loving service, know this best of all. Giving freely blesses the giver as well as the recipient. Don't put conditions on your giving that will only lead to disappointment and unrealized expectations. Find new ways to extend your love.

Included among those new ways could be modest, but loving comments, going the extra mile to performed tasks not essential to your caregiving duties, employing complimentary suggestions rather than condemning remarks, listening more attentively and truly seeking to understand your loved one, open dialogue about previously unmentioned and unresolved issues, do little things to remind both of you your affection in the past, satisfying unfulfilled requests, reading a book together, sharing your ideas and thoughts, discovering unknown things about each other, etc. The list is endless, and so are the rewards.

Fourthly, Discover What Unconditional Love Looks Like

THERE ARE MANY TYPES of love and real love in life today can be hard to define. From poets, to psychologists, to everyday people, the endless effort to explain what love is and means beyond "you know it when you feel it" has led to innumerable thoughts and ideas. For me, there is one tried and true definition of unconditional love I often refer back to. That's God's example to us. No matter what your stance on religion may be, the wise description of unconditional love is given in I Corinthians 13 in the Bible. This definition is simple, yet profoundly effective if taken to heart and put into action. Love is patient, kind, does not envy, does not boast, is not proud, is not rude, is not self-seeking, is not easily angered, keeps no record of wrongs, does not delight in evil but rejoices in truth, always protects, trusts, hopes, and perseveres. It never fails. Love is more important than anything else. These characteristics show what unconditional love is. You will find some of those truths in the thoughts below.

Unconditional Love Makes Giving Love More-Important Than Anything Else.
It Means a Person Is More Important <u>Than Your Expectations</u>

EXPECTATIONS ARE JUST YOUR requirements for "acceptability" of loving someone. But true love has no expectations. It simply loves "as is."

Unconditional Love Doesn't Play The <u>Victim Role or Blame Others</u>

LOVE DOESN'T THINK THEIR loved ones are evilly wrong. Love works together for the good of both people. It takes responsibility rather than blames. It forgives and allows other people's actions to be *their* journey in life and not a personal affront against one's self. Love doesn't take things personally. Even if someone doesn't apologize, it's inherently loving to both parties to let go of anger and resentment before it can poison the relationship. Keep in mind Piero Ferrucci's advice that forgiving *is not something we do, but something we are.* If someone you love says something hurtful in anger, the loving choice is to let him know the words hurt you, but also to forgive his indiscretion. Help the other person to understand and grow, continue to love him unconditionally, and seek to understand where your partner is on his journey in life.

Unconditional Love Is an Action, Not Just a Feeling

HUMANS TEND TO BE addicted to intense emotion — especially when it feels good. So, when we're in love, we want to feel that way forever. When that "in love" feeling goes away, it doesn't mean you don't love the other person anymore, it just means that your feelings are not new anymore. So that's when the action needs to kick in. Emotions and feelings will fluctuate throughout life. Love is action not a feeling, which means love is a choice a person makes minute by minute every day.

Unconditional Love Is Actually Unconditional

THE WORD "UNCONDITIONAL" MEANS that there are no expectations or limitations set. To love unconditionally is a difficult thing, and most humans aren't good at that. But true love really does love without trying to change the other person.

Unconditional Love Means Putting Other People's Needs Equal To — Or Before — Your Own

LOVED ONES MAY BE inherently selfish for survival purposes; this does not serve us well in relationships. If you don't put other people's needs at least equal to your own, they will grow resentful and lose trust in the relationship. Real love truly, genuinely cares about other people's happiness.

Unconditional Love Requires Attention

LOVE DOESN'T IGNORE. IT doesn't look the other way. It wants to be present and be together. When people are in love, sometimes they think that they don't have to "do any more work." But real love actually enjoys giving attention to another person. It feels good.

Unconditional Love Understands and Accepts Differences

LET'S FACE IT, WE'RE all different. Even identical twins aren't exactly the same. They have different experiences and outlooks about the world. Real love doesn't make other people wrong for being different. When people truly love other persons, they accept their differences. A large part of accepting others is not expecting them to make you happy through the choices they make and how they live out their journey in life. You can't control others, only yourself. Love is about what we give not what we get.

Unconditional Love Varies in How It Is Expressed And Accepted

WHAT MAKES US "FEEL loved" varies. It's important to discover other people's love language so you can understand each other and give love in a way the other person recognizes it.

Unconditional Love Makes You
<u>Feel Good, Not Bad</u>

MANY PEOPLE CONFUSE BEING in a relationship with love. Just because you're in a relationship doesn't mean there is true love present. If there is jealousy, possessiveness, constant fighting, abuse (verbal, emotional or physical), that is not love.

<u>Unconditional Love Has Empathy</u>

EMPATHY IS THE ABILITY to put yourself into another person's shoes and see a situation from his/her point of view. Love has deep empathy. People who truly love one another don't want to hurt each other. They want another to feel good. They care about the other one's feelings and wants the other to feel valued. (17)

<u>Fifthly, Love Yourself Unconditionally</u>

UNCONDITIONAL LOVE STARTS AT home, with oneself. You know your own flaws and shortcomings better than anyone else, and better than you can ever know anyone else's. Being able to love yourself despite this unsurpassable awareness of your own faults, puts you in the position to offer the same love to your ill loved one.

Realizing you are worthy and unique and beautiful just as you are is crucial to accepting other people. Otherwise your own insecurities will rule your actions and your love. Sometimes, this means forgiving yourself for past mistakes, too. What hidden parts of yourself are keeping you from having a joyful life? What is keeping you in the prison of your past?

You need to face those things about yourself and free yourself to a new future. To truly love and forgive others, you must have the heart and the courage to love and forgive yourself. You don't have to be perfect to love somebody, just be honest.

Lastly, Realize Unconditional Love Is Not Being "Blinded" By Love

A PERSON WHO HAS newly fallen in love with another is often in this state, where he/she does not see the other person's full reality, faults and all. Such a state of love is (or at least should be) temporary, and needs to be replaced by a longer-term, "eyes wide open" type of love if the love is to last.

With your eyes wide open, you can identify negatives that will harmfully influence your feelings for your loved one over time. This approach enables you to see both the good as well as the not so good aspects of your loved one's personality and behavior. You can then make a conscious choice to be more appreciative of one's positives as well as prepare yourself for all negative eventualities. Being forewarned is being forearmed. Unconditional love accepts and absorbs those unplanned occurrences. Being flexible and willing to make allowances for the humanity of your loved one expands your love and makes the caregiving experience for you and your loved one a joyful time.

Part of eyes wide open love is realizing you cannot shield someone you love from all discomfort and pain. Allowing them to grow as a person is important. Pain and discomfort are inescapable parts of life. Unconditional love means doing what you can to make the other person happy and comfortable, but also allowing them to grow through their inevitable experiences of discomfort and supporting them along the way.

Because of the many and continual physical difficulties and pain experienced by my wife, Wendy, I discussed the possible connection of discomfort to unconditional love. I wanted to know if from the patient's view, did that discomfort cause an expected or natural loss of love? As always, she was right on point. Convincingly she said:

> *Through much discomfort and concern I have found it necessary to nurture love, love for self and love for partner. I know I must concentrate on the positive and discuss in depth any negative experiences or feelings. Developing a loving relationship, combined with achieving personal spirituality, should be a person's lifetime work. I believe that no unpleasant physical or emotional obstacles should change that endeavor. My life is based on preserving and enjoying our time and love together. Despite my physical discomforts, I enjoy my life and love my husband.*

FINAL COMMENTS ABOUT
<u>THE ULTIMATE TEST</u>

UNCONDITIONAL LOVE CAN GROW with time. Love honors effort. For those who feel their love slipping or gone, "get back on the horse." Try not to be a casualty to your fatigue or struggle. Developing unconditional love will ease your burdens, and improve your attitude. What you do, and what you are matter. Your unconditional love will certainly mean the world to your loved one.

I want to leave you with one final thought.

The Last Kiss

A GOOD FRIEND, KNOWING about the writing of this book, passed along this very touching story about his tender last moments with his dying wife. His story is a clear beacon to all who feel that their romance is slipping, or their love for the patient is nearly gone.

His experience touched me, and I hope will touch you, too. I hope his tenderness will motivate you to re-examine your life and work on your relationship with your loved one:

This night was no different than hundreds of other nights of our being together. My sweetheart of over fifty years was sitting on our bed as she could no longer kneel down because of her illness. I was kneeling with my arms around her waist; we bowed our heads in silent prayer – a habit we had adopted on the day that we were wed. Then we kissed; two kisses, also a tradition.

After prayers were said, we lay silently side by side holding hands, a custom we had also enjoyed those many years together, even during the many years of her illness. Then she turned to me and asked, "May I have one more kiss?" I answered with another kiss. This was different – three kisses? How wonderful!

The next day, she was gone. I had not realized the third kiss was her goodbye kiss. But somehow, she knew. How much we should treasure each goodnight kiss! We never know when, do we?

10.

THE HOPE

A pessimist sees the difficulty in every opportunity; the optimist sees the opportunity in every difficulty.
– Winston Churchill

———————— ⸸ ————————

ATTEMPTING TO BRING ABOUT an attitude of optimism can, in fact, bring it about. What you think, say, do, and hope for is what you become. Being optimistic is worth working on. It is unlikely that your loved one will miss your increased efforts to be optimistic. It should be contagious! If it is, hope will not be lost; and, it too may become contagious.

Hope Is Being Optimistic

WINSTON CHURCHILL, THE EXTRAORDINARY Prime Minister of Great Britain during World War II, was a perfect example of an individual whose words and actions enabled others to stay optimistic and dare to believe that good could come out of difficult circumstances. He had a way that shouted out optimism. He knew what to say and do and he said and did it. One day while asked about how he could be such an optimist during such dark days, he replied "didn't seem much use being anything else."

The war certainly provided Sir Winston Churchill the stage, but my guess is that individuals like Winston Churchill would have found another stage if it hadn't been for the war. We each have a stage. It has been provided for us. It is our relationships with family, our friends, our neighbors, our associates, and others who do or could believe in us. We can be optimistic like Sir Winston. We can use our stage for presenting a more positive view of all things, particularly about our caregiving responsibilities.

But the matter-at-hand is the care of our loved ones, patients suffering from disease or injury. It is imperative that we be optimistic for them, even when we might not feel optimistic. Attempting to bring about an attitude of optimism can, in fact, bring it about. We become what we think about and what we say and do. Being optimistic is worth working on. Your loved one will not miss your increased efforts to be optimistic. It may even be contagious!

Hope Is Being Positive

BE CAREFUL TO NEVER let the sickness or injury of your loved one destroy your hope – or your patient's hope. The message is hope, but the foundation of that hope is preparation. Find out what you need to know in order to be fully prepared. Far too many cases studied revealed an alarming lack of hope exhibited by those who were providing care for their critically and terminally ill loved ones who, in many cases, have also become sadly negative, frustrated and hopeless. Logic suggests that these attitudes will eventually rub off on each other, causing hope to dwindle for both of you. That doesn't have to happen.

> *Hope is an optimistic attitude of mind that is based on an expectation of positive outcomes related to events and circumstances in one's life or the world at large. As a verb, its definitions include: "expect with confidence" and "to cherish a desire with anticipation". Among its opposites are dejection, hopelessness and despair. (7)*

Hope Is Comforting and Motivating

THE MERRIAM-WEBSTER DICTIONARY SAYS that hope is: "to want something to happen or be true and think that it could happen or be true . . . or cherish a desire with anticipation . . . to desire with expectation of obtainment." (12).

The definition pertains to the short term. My experience with hope is long term. I have always focused on long term objectives. That focus was easy with hope. Hope provides a clarity and a direction that helps make decisions and efforts effective. Hope shouldn't vanish with difficulty or hardship. Hope, very possibly, can come to an individual easier than expected and stay longer than originally thought.

Hope Is Valuable In the Healing Process

HOPE IS LIKE FAITH. It provides strength in a moment of weakness and determination when faced with difficult odds. Hope has been a continual reinforcement for my life. Hope has provided peace when it was most needed. Wikipedia, in discussing how valuable hope is in the healing process, says this about hope:

> *Hope has the ability to help people heal faster and easier. Individuals who maintain hope, especially when battling illness, significantly enhance their chances of recovery.*

This is important because numerous people with chronic, physical, or mental illness believe that their condition is, at best, stable and that they have little chance of recovery. If health care providers begin to recognize the importance of hope in the recovery process, they can learn to instill hope within their patients. This would enable patients to develop healthy coping strategies and therefore improve their physical and emotional wellbeing.

Shaping people's beliefs and expectations to be more hopeful and optimistic is an essential component of positive psychology. In general, people who possess hope and think optimistically have a greater sense of well-being in addition to the improved health outcomes outlined above. Positive psychologists teach strategies to help boost people's hope and optimism, which would benefit individuals coping with illness by improving their satisfaction and recovery process.

Love Helps Preserve Hope

MANY FAITHFUL CAREGIVERS WHO, by no fault of their own, are stuck in a seemingly, hopeless medical ordeal. It is about hope – hope for the caregiver and hope for the patient. Sickness can have an oppressive effect on those most closely involved. If a caregiver's hope is now missing or slipping then the issue becomes restoring hope. Hope can be restored. Hope is the result of positive thinking. Hope is like love, it invigorates and uplifts. Hope is necessary and healthy for both the caregiver and the recipient.

Believe You Will Be Strong

STRENGTH CAN COME FROM actions other than exercise and lifting weights. There is emotional and psychological strength. It may one day be necessary to draw strength from all of these sources. Certainly, caregiving can be physically exhausting, but so can it be emotionally tiring. The pressure to perform, and to be decisive, is difficult for some individuals. Everyone can draw strength from available actions such as exercise and proper eating. Strength can come from associating with positive people. Identify those most apt to be of assistance and seize available opportunities. Be the first to notice that you need hope and how you best can obtain it. Overcoming the fear of not succeeding and/or surviving can be exhilarating.

Believe You Will Survive

CAREGIVERS ARE USED TO giving their all. The medical necessities demand that certain actions be taken. Over time it wears on the caregiver. I have spoken with caregivers who feared they might not live long enough to finish providing the necessary care for their loved ones. It is hard to imagine that providing service to someone who is ill would be so physically demanding. While the physical requirements are demanding, the emotional pressure of medical responsibility also takes its' toll.

The fear of making a mistake, or missing a feeding, or failing to provide medicine on time, etc. are all complicating pressures.

Caretakers relate they fear they will not be physically well enough to survive. Occasionally they doubt any desire to survive. Let that not be you! There is always something you can do to lift your will to survive.

Believe You Will Remain Hopeful

HOPEFUL COMES FROM THE word hope, meaning "optimism about a future event." So, if you're hopeful, you're full of hope: You think something good is going to happen. You might be hopeful that you'll be offered something valuable soon. Hopeful can describe a promising person who wants to succeed at a particular goal. You can be that person. The goal for caregiving is providing comfort and care to a loved one that will lead to recovery or an extended life. Despite the fatigue, loneliness and frustration, hope can be the ultimate and eventual strength for survival. Take a rest but never give up. There will always be something to hope for. There will always be things you can do. There will always be joy in succeeding.

Believe Good Things Will Happen

IT IS DIFFICULT TO believe that good things are going to happen when bad things keep occurring. That is all the more reason to have hope and believe good things will happen. Good things just might happen, and even if they don't, believing good things could happen just might get you through the difficult times.

After her own challenging experiences, Goldei wrote the following:

If you say or even think you can't do something, then you won't. It's that simple. And this is the saddest truth there is in the process of being successful. There are so many hurdles you will face in your journey to wherever it is that you're going, there's no getting around it. There will be plenty of circumstances and people and limits that you will face insisting that you can't. NO matter how positive, how motivated or how successful you become, there will always be obstacles in your way, it's just a natural part in the process. However, the biggest obstacle you will likely face is yourself. I can pretty much guarantee the only thing standing between you and your most outlandish dreams and goals are the limits you place on yourself. You can accomplish almost anything you can dream of with the right tools and motivation. But you will not accomplish even your most ordinary goals if you say you can't. You will never know how hard, or how easy something really is until you actually try with all your might if you never even give it a chance. "Can't" is the ultimate serial killer of Chance. You might not even be aware that you are you're own worst enemy, and how much you are limiting yourself simply by your own conviction that you can't . . . You CAN do it." (1)

Believe in Uplifting Others

THIS IS A TOUGH principle. Difficult as it might be, lifting others when you don't feel uplifted yourself is not easy. It can even feel a little hypocritical, but at times it may be necessary. Lifting a loved one who is dying or trapped in a long bedridden experience is tougher. Complicating the issue, as you know, is the fact that 56% of the reported caregivers in the NAC/AARP study simply are feeling less love for the recipient of the care and that makes adopting an uplifting attitude all the more difficult. (6)

We all want good things to happen, and it really is possible with a good attitude, and an uplifting personality. We can change the attitudes and inclination of those around us by the utilization of the principle of hope. An uplifting attitude is a hopeful attitude.

I found the following lines during my research, but failed to record the reference. Hopefully, should the author read these lines, I can be forgiven:

> *The simple feeling of hope is the feeling of wanting something to happen and thinking that it could happen. Hope is a feeling that something good will happen or be true. Hope is believing that someone or something may be able to provide help. Hope is someone or something that gives you a reason for hoping.*

Hope is Lifesaving.

CERTAINLY, THOSE WHO ARE discouraged need someone. If that someone who needs hope is you, take the steps found in this short-book to regenerate your hope! If it is your loved one patient who needs hope, determine that you will be someone who will help raise the uplifting feeling of hope for him.

Below you will find the story of a woman who had reasons to be discouraged but, due to her never-ending hope, never gave up:

> *My husband of 46 years has Parkinson's disease. He used to walk 4-plus miles to the hospital where he was a cardiologist. Now he's exhausted in less than one city block. But we do it! Every day! His parkinsonian moods can make him depressingly (for both of us) down. And his needs are so many I had no time for my own*

pleasures as I did in the past. But now I feel a deep content inside seeing him try so hard to walk down by the Hudson River and reward him by reading his chosen articles from the papers to him out loud while he munches on a sandwich. It seems idyllic. I am so grateful. I was a very busy science editor for years. I had a life of travel, twice a year to Paris and other places. Now we cannot travel and I feel a peace within. I thank God when I am feeling just too tired to go on. And then I relax and can go to sleep. I wake up happy. And I feel so privileged to be the one to watch over my husband. I keep strong by exercising down by the river while he completes his own walk holding onto the rail by the river. As bad as it is that he is in this condition, we are in love and excited about our life. I could not do it without the miracles that God has placed in our lives, and I am constantly in a state of grace. God saved his life after a fall he had 4 years ago, and I will never let him down. (1)

How To Maintain Hope

CAREGIVERS NEED POWERFUL SUGGESTIONS for developing and strengthening hope. Any of the previous suggestions will help. In addition, there are a few other principles which are known to work well and could be recommended to the readers of this book because they might help those who feel hope is lost or slipping away.

Making progress in the areas listed below may change
a caregiver's life and future outlook:

Develop Meaning In Your Life

DO YOU OFTEN FIND yourself struggling to see any meaning or purpose in your day-to-day activities? Do you want to break out of bad habits but can't find the desire to do so? Hope might seem like a vague word with perhaps little to no relevance in your life, but insofar as it means seeing the possibilities inherent to your life, it might just be the precursor for you to get out of the rut you are in.

Prepare for the Day Things Get Better

SO MANY OF US get discouraged and lose hope as a result. Although disappointments are natural, there is nothing natural about living a "less-than" life. Internalize this: The funny thing about change is; it happens in an instant. For days, weeks, years, things stay the same, and then one day they're not. You won't be down forever, so prepare for that day, now. Hopefulness is gained by knowing that this too shall pass, and by getting ready for the day that it does. (9)

Hope Brightens Our Charity for Others

PRESIDENT DIETER F. UCHTDORF had the following to say about how hope braces our resolve and urges us to care for our patients in an extended and tender manner.

When disobedience, disappointment, and procrastination erode faith, hope is there to uphold our faith. When frustration and impatience challenge charity, hope braces our resolve and urges us to care for our fellowmen even without expectation of reward. The brighter our hope, the greater is our faith. The stronger our hope, the purer is our charity. (10)

Hanging on To Hope

CLARITY POINT COACH, KRISTENA Eden, interviewed inmates from the Utah State Penitentiary recently to talk about hanging on to hope (since prison is a place where life often feels hopeless). These are some other key principles that came to light.

1. KEEP BELIEVING THERE *is a light at the end of the tunnel.* Allow room in your heart for dreaming about better times. It is easy to let our dreams go because we just feel they are impossible or we are not good enough to accomplish them. But take a look around your world today. All the amazing technology and the conveniences we now enjoy were at one time thought to be impossible. If you can dream, then you can hang onto hope.

2. GIVE SINCERE ENCOURAGEMENT *to others.* This is a big one. Giving encouragement to others is one of the greatest ways to validate them and make them feel valued. You don't have to agree with what they are choosing in their life, but a few minutes to just ask questions and listen to them can make a world of difference. When other people feel that you care about them, they feel better and you do too.

3. REPLACE DESTRUCTIVE THOUGHTS *with positive ones.* Your thoughts are the building blocks of your quality of life. Your thoughts become feelings, so you want to monitor your thinking and recognize when negative thoughts show up, you have the power and agency to embrace them or replace them.

4. BE AN OVER-COMER, *not just a survivor.* A survivor is still a victim, an over-comer is a victor who understands it was just a lesson and you were meant to get through. Over-comers don't complain about the hardship forever because they leave it in the past.

5. FOCUS ON GRATITUDE. It doesn't matter how bad things seem, they could be worse. There are always things to be grateful for. Sometimes it's things you are grateful you don't have, as much as it is for what you do have.

6. KEEP YOUR CONFIDENCE, *you are meant to overcome this.* You are not in this place to fail or be crushed. You are here to grow and meant to find solutions, courage and strength to get through. The answers you need are around you somewhere, but they may require work and effort to find and only when your lesson is done. For now, stay solution focused and ask for help from every resource and person that shows up in your path.

FINAL COMMENTS ON HOPE

NEVER GIVE UP! NEVER give up hope! Never give up hope for achieving real happiness! Hope and happiness are enabling powers that allow individuals to have the courage to keep going, to look for better ways, to encourage others and to believe – believe in yourself and in others. Hope is the safety cord that when pulled enables individuals to hang on when others feel hope is lost. Dare to believe that through your efforts and your hope, you can bring about any desired result you seek. Good things will happen. Never, ever, give up hope! Never, ever, give up on yourself or your patient! Love is the doorway to that kind of hope and happiness.

11.

THE HAPPINESS

*Happiness is when what you think, what you say, and what you do
are in harmony*
– Mahatma Ghandi

AFTER 40 YEARS OF research, social scientists attribute happiness to
three major sources: genes, events, and values. Armed with this knowledge, and a few simple rules, we can improve our lives and the lives of
those around us. We can even construct a system that fulfills our found-
ers' promises and empowers all Americans to pursue happiness. (16)

Happiness is different for almost everyone and can be allusive, un-
defined, and unrecognized. Happiness is sought by the lonely and those
who are not lonely. It is exhilarating and uplifting. For some it changes
personalities and attitudes. For those who don't know happiness, they
grieve for it, as if they've lost a loved one. Happiness, like love, is a
companion - you know when it is present and miss it when it is gone.

As Ghandi indicated, happiness is a state of being created by a match between our spiritual journey and our human experience – it means we are on the right track. All people want to find happiness, but not all of us find it, because our spiritual well-being and growth is in discord with our day to day actions. We either don't know where to look for harmony within our own hearts and minds, or don't know how to achieve it.

Perhaps the best answer isn't found inside of ourselves.

Unique Definition of Happiness

I HAVE GROWN IMPRESSED with a young man, a high school senior, in our neighborhood. He is always smiling, seems positive, obviously intelligent and remarkably diligent. Included in a talk he made recently to the entire body of his church was this remarkable definition of happiness:

> *Happiness leaves no bad after-taste. It is followed by no de-pressing reaction; it calls for no repentance, brings no regret, entails no remorse; true happiness is lived over and over again in memory; always with a renewal of the original good; (however) a moment of unholy pleasure may leave a barbed sting, which like a thorn in the flesh, is an ever-present source of anguish.* (13)

This definition will be memorable for me. If internalized by care-givers, it will stand the test of time. It avoids modern hyperbole, and it reminds me of my young friend.

Throughout this Short-Book I have emphasized uplifting attri-butes and introduced safeguards to void falling into hopelessness and depression. Happiness just doesn't magically happen in anyone's life. It is something you must seek and fight to have. No person, situation, or material thing can bring you true happiness. And no one person, situation, or lack of material thing can take happiness away. Happiness is a state of being generated by the perspective you choose to have about life and the response you choose to face life with. But, when you gain happiness in your own life, it becomes infectious, and can bring joy to everyone around you. (16)

Understanding this foundation is key to the rest of this chapter. Here are a few stepping stones toward choosing your path to happiness.

Making Each Other Happy

TO ACHIEVE LASTING PERSONAL happiness, most caregivers will need to help their loved ones gain their personal happiness as well. This will take a lot of work. In order to accomplish both, the relationship will need to be filled with an attitude of love, cooperation, acceptance, and forgiveness. Usually, it requires a commitment on the part of both people to make each other happy. In some cases, though, the commitment may rest exclusively with the caregiver. That shouldn't stop caregivers from seeking a harmonious relationship with their loved one – keep working at it, and you likely will succeed.

Loving Care

THE MERRIAM WEBSTER DICTIONARY defines loving care as: "extra attention to make someone or something look or feel better." Their emphasis is on "extra attention" which means that additional efforts must be expended to make a difference in the relationship and bring about the changes in attitudes required to finding mutual happiness.

Happiness doesn't require perfection, but it does need a consistently tender and loving attitude toward your partner. The constant application of positive unconditional love will produce the desired, harmonious, happy relationship every couple dreams of having. When your partner truly realizes you can be counted on physically and emotionally, they are more likely to entrust their heart to you. When they know, you will do what you say you will do and will always be loving, the bonds of a truly harmonious relationship strengthen and grow.

Making a Difference Means Learning New Skills

I AM NOT SURE if it's just my perception of the world, but there seems to be a serious lack of nice lately, a deficit in kindness and respect. Some individuals are simply nice. They just naturally do the right, kind, and loving thing, and make a difference because of it. For the rest of us, nice and kind in trying and well as normal circumstances doesn't come easy. We must learn how to be nice.

While serving as an officer of a competing department store, I happened to be talking to Bruce Nordstrom of Nordstrom's, a fashion store, headquartered in Seattle, WA. I asked him how they get their sales people to be so nice and give such good customer service. He said, "We don't hire good sales people and teach them to be nice, we hire nice people and teach them how to sell."

The world would benefit if all its inhabitants made the conscious effort to be nice. If you want to make a difference in your relationships and the world, you will have to learn the skills. Being nice and respectful in all circumstances, going the extra mile to make your loved one feel appreciated will bring you both joy.

Pleasure and Satisfaction

HAVE YOU EVER MADE a list of what pleases you? I suggest you and your loved one do just that. You will be surprised to find, you'll both have some of the same items on the list. But would either of you include making others happy on that list? Would it include developing harmonious aspects to your own personality and attitude? Would it include pleasing others with your comments, smiles, and acts?

Finding real joy and happiness in life means becoming aware of what brings pleasure and satisfaction to others, and giving freely to them.

This should be especially true in the caregiving situation with a loved one. Joy should come from making the other person happy.

So why do so many people fail to achieve real happiness?

Have you ever met a person who doesn't want to be happy? No, right? Happiness is like the Holy Grail of life – the ultimate goal and desire of every human being. Because happiness, feeling good spiritually, and being physically active are interconnected by our emotions. We want real and uplifting lives. We are wired to love feeling good.

Sounds like a no-brainer for everyone to act and make choices designed to achieve real happiness in life, but we don't.

Many times, we do the exact opposite and we treat the ones we love poorly.

Your life does not have to be filled with sadness and dissatisfaction.

You can change. By becoming what we need to be for others, we become who we need to be for ourselves. The more you love others, you unlock the door to happiness in your own life.

Why Practice Being Happy?

ACACIA PARKS, PhD, STATED in *What Is Happiness, Anyway?*

> *Happiness is a combination of how satisfied you are with your life (for example, finding meaning in your work) and how good you feel on a day-to-day basis.*

How we feel about our life is extremely important, but regardless of how satisfied we are or how good we feel, happiness should be, and often is, the by-product of how we treat each other. I have come to believe the more we do for each other, the happier we will both be. Is it possible that the happier our loved one becomes, the happier we will become? I think so! Happiness comes with effort, and it is an inestimable prize worth working hard to achieve. And, happiness is nearly always the by-product of a loving relationship.

In addition to making us feel good, studies have found that happiness actually improves other aspects of our lives. Here is an overview of some of the good stuff that research has linked to happiness:

Happiness is good for our health. There's research to suggest people who have a more positive outlook are less likely to get sick after being exposed to flu and cold viruses. And, a recent study suggests getting a hug from a loved one can also fight off viruses such as the common cold. While that one is hard to believe, why not try it? Happiness does produce good hormones in our bodies. Surely, that has a positive effect on every aspect of our daily life.

Those who rate higher on certain positive personality traits have lower rates of certain illnesses.

For instance, one study found people who were more agreeable, extraverted, open, and conscientious, all had lower risks of developing illnesses such as cancer and diabetes. The researchers found that conscientiousness in particular could have a protective effect against health problems. So, reviewing what modern research is saying about happy people:

Happy people are less likely to get sick, and they live longer.

Happiness is good for our relationships:

Happy people are more likely to get married and have fulfilling marriages.

Happy people have more friends.

Happy people make more money and are more productive at work.

Happy people are more generous.

Happy people cope better with stress and trauma.

Happy people are more creative and are better able to see the big picture.

Happy people are more grateful and in tune with their spiritual self.

Happy people are kind to others and make a difference everywhere they go.

How Much Do You Want Happiness?

EVERY INDIVIDUAL MUST DECIDE what they want from life. What makes for happiness and how to achieve joy is usually a part of that decision. Yet, for many, especially caregivers, happiness seems too elusive to consider. Can I tell you if you believe something is impossible, it is likely you will never achieve it? No matter what your situation, there is something you can do to improve it.

Just simply deciding what you really want and what you are willing to sacrifice to obtain it can be a game changer in life. That includes happiness.

How bad do you want it? Do you want the hurt to go away for both you and your loved one?

If so, decide today you will do something to make happiness happen for you both. What are you willing to do to accomplish your goal?

Determine nothing will stop you, or prevent you from achieving happiness in your life.

This will include your relationships, feelings, actions. It will mean eliminating conduct and emotions standing in your way.

Happiness can be had, but it must be fought for wearing the armament of love if you want to win the battle.

Ways to Enhance Happiness

WHILE HAPPINESS IS DEFINED by an individual's choice, it seems foolish to declare nothing can be learned from observing the happiness of others. Wisdom suggests that by examining and observing the happy patterns of others, and then taking only what is useful, one's life can be significantly better. Loving and tender care should be the goal, not rigid rules on being happy.

Think of Yourself Less

HUMILITY IS NOT THINKING less of yourself, but thinking of yourself less. Having a good self-esteem means you understand God's love and your worth to Him and humbly realize He values other people just as dearly. This is not to be confused with ego, which values self over others.

We think less about ourselves when we observe what makes other people happy. In fact, on a personal note, sometimes I have experienced greater satisfaction and happiness when seeing joy brought into the life of someone else. This can be true for confined loved ones. They can experience the joy of others if we surround them with other people, rather than leave them isolated in their illness.

Be Productive, but Not Busy or Rushed

SET YOUR AGENDA WITH your priorities and goals in mind. Give yourself a reasonable amount of time in which to accomplish them and build in free time for yourself and an exercise regimen, too. By establishing a steady routine of productive living, you will end each day satisfied with the progress you have made. Being overly busy without the results you desire, will cause stress and unhappiness. On the other hand, underachieving, and having too little to do, may also bring about depression and unhappiness.

In recent studies, psychologists claim that people with the ability to set objectives for themselves – both short-term and long-term – are happier. Additional research backs up this finding: goals really do add a sense of meaning, direction, and focus to life that can easily become absent if we don't have anything for which we are currently striving.

Including exercise is vital. There is no getting around it. Even if you hate exercise, there are so many benefits for it (both physically and psychologically) that you should be doing it regularly in some form. To add to the pile, research has also found exercise is a proven strategy for feeling better, increasing your energy levels, and reducing tension.

Finding the happy medium of being just busy enough is an important step in establishing and keeping happiness.

Have Five Close Relationships

RELATIONSHIPS ARE PERHAPS THE most important thing (without exaggeration) when it comes to overall life satisfaction, at least for most people. Having a close group of people in your life can keep you happy for life (it can also help you live longer). National surveys find that when someone claims to have five or more friends with whom they can discuss important problems, they are 60 percent more likely to say that they are "very happy."

Keep Moving Forward

LIVE IN THE PRESENT and not the past. Let go of mistakes, and the "could haves, should haves, and would haves," in life and in relationships.

I have heard it said relationships are not static. They are either growing or declining. Growth requires pro-action and action. Plan it and do it. Relationships (especially marriages) decline over time. You have to plan to keep love alive and then follow through with actions focused on keeping your love and friendship dynamic and meaningful.

While spontaneous fun is always a good thing, a variety of interesting research has shown it's the planning of future activities that often adds to the fun. While the study above specifically looked at vacations (which may not occur often), additional research revealed that specifically planning a nice dinner can have the same effect. Caregiving may inhibit some events, but shouldn't ever negate this. There are always special things to hope for and to be done.

Part of moving forward means you can't remain static either. Striving for your own personal development, and sharing your new knowledge in a loving, caring manner will enrich everyone's life. So, pick a skill and master it. Excellence in anything increases your potential in everything. As it turns out, regularly engaging in your strengths is a great way to feel better about yourself. The long and short of it is, you should find something to excel in, and do it as often as you can. Increase your ability to love and keep it moving forward, too. It's almost unimaginable how much good can be accomplish with dynamic love.

Move Beyond the Small Talk

"GREAT MINDS DISCUSS IDEAS; average minds discuss events; small minds discuss people." Eleanor Roosevelt's quote has certainly made its' rounds on many a Facebook feed, but is there any truth to it? The extent of small talk was negatively associated with happiness . . . .and the extent of substantive talk was positively associated with happiness. So, happy people are socially engaged with others, and this engagement entails matters of substance. Deep conversations are often those we reserve for close friends and family, which explains why close, loving relationships are so important for happiness.

Treat Yourself (The Small Pleasures Matter)

WISDOM ALSO SUGGESTS THAT you need to have small wins along the way in order to maintain happiness. So, it is important to reward yourself with something special to you. Happiness is more strongly associated with the frequency of positive experiences than the intensity of them.

Keep Your Eye on the Prize

YOU'VE LIKELY HEARD OF the marshmallow experiment, but a quick summary is: researchers have found children who were able to resist the temptation of eating a marshmallow immediately (vs. waiting for the researchers to come back) did notably better in some major areas of life, leaving some to conclude that delayed gratification is a solid predictor of future success. The research has shown a connection between delayed gratification and overall life satisfaction. People with self-control live a happier life.

Show Some Appreciation

HAVING GRATITUDE FOR SOMEONE (or even for what you have) boosted happiness by a noticeable level. The researchers say by as much as 25%. This includes positive communications with people in your life. Thank you notes, nice letters, encouraging and uplifting messages on social media, all of it works for the benefit of others and for yourself.

In one study researchers found that the simple act of listing three good things that happen each day (no matter how small) increased happiness and decreased depressive symptoms. Furthermore, putting yourself in someone else' shoes (and avoiding a pessimistic outlook) really can make you feel better about your situation. A change in perspective can have a big impact on your overall happiness.

Don't Let Time Slip Away

WE LOSE SO MUCH every day because we let time pass us by without making good use of it. Apart from maintaining strong relationships, ending procrastination is one of the most important steps to maintaining happiness, bar none. Time is precious and can never be recaptured. Use it to its ultimate advantage. Do something every day of which you can be proud.

FINAL COMMENTS ABOUT HAPPINESS

IT IS HARD TO remember and go back to the positive emotions and affections of earlier times. Many can't or won't do it, but realize happiness is a choice everyone has the complete power to make. I know, for caregivers with a difficult physical and/or emotional trial, happiness feels almost impossible, and out of reach. But it isn't. Yes, effort will be required, faith will be helpful, and love essential. But if you make the choice, that whatever happiness takes, it must happen. That the relationship, as difficult as it might be, matters more than any of the obstacles preventing it from improving. That love is the answer and loving is the process. Happiness for all will be the ultimate reward, because happiness can change hearts and lives.

Choose for it to change yours.

12.

ABOUT COURAGE

Being deeply loved by someone gives you strength, while loving some-one deeply gives you courage.
– ANONYMOUS

———————— ⸎ ————————

ARE YOU READY TO change your life?

Are you anxious to end burdening emotional stress?

Do you have courage?

Is your heart crying out, yes! I want these things, but in your mind, you think you can't do any more than you already are?

Are you unsure of what courage is?

I have a secret to share. Courage isn't always some superhuman feat of extraordinary action. Simply put, courage is making a choice to do what is right in the face of your fear, or hardship, or overwhelming circumstance.

Consider stories about miraculous acts of strength in desperate moments—such as a mother lifting a car off her child. When her child faced danger and death, the mother didn't think I can't do this, or this is impossible to do alone. She acted. With instinct, courage, and love she rescued her child.

Is it a miracle when something like this happens? Or, did the mother's belief she could save her child, did in fact, save him?

Caregivers who step in and rescue loved ones are no less heroic. Their act of courage isn't a dramatic event publicized to the world, but an everyday choice to lift and carry the burden of a loved one's wellbeing. Being brave is not only for war heroes, but also for normal people doing their very best. Miraculous? Courageous? I think so. You have chosen right in the face of hardship by becoming a caretaker. So, can you now see that making a choice for happiness and joy is possible?

Few personal or public victories are won without making difficult and painful decisions then following through on those choices with sacrifice and action. This recipe for success applies to achieving happiness and love in relationships, too, even in caregiving circumstances.

Below are my thoughts on uncovering, discovering, and developing courage in your life. They are important ones and worth reiterating through the perspective of courage in your life.

Remember, by being a caretaker, you already are a hero with great courage and you can make your life one of joy, happiness and love.

Have the Courage to Ask and Believe

I KNOW I ASKED for a miracle when nine first responders worked so diligently to save my wife, Wendy. Whether I asked for it properly or not in my panic, a miracle resulted and our lives remained blessed to this day. Miracles do happen. Individuals are helped, lifted, and saved in many different ways every day.

Throughout my life, in prayer, I've asked for miracles. Sometimes those things occur. Sometimes they do not. But over the years, a confidence and hope have grown as I have seen many times goodness and happiness rise up from desperate circumstances. Asking for the joy of happiness, asking for love to be found and not lost is just as important as any other request.

I have read hundreds of stories from caregivers expressing serious and real emotional worries. They relate the grief and the stress they are experiencing from their caregiving troubles. These problems are not make-believe, and combine to leave the caregiver in a state of hopelessness, or with an attitude of self-pity. Forgive me for that harsh assessment, but unless an individual can face what is happening, he or she can't change it. This is not a criticism, but is a real result of what happens when caregivers feel they have been placed in an impossible position.

Life is never fair. Life is full of struggle and each person has their own burdens to carry. The only way to overcome the trouble you face is to move forward. To see past the pain and difficulty by putting your goals and focus on what you want your life to become.

Feeling sorry for one's self or resentful or your circumstances will be counter-productive to your life and rob you of the very love and happiness you desire.

That being said, we are back to the simple truth we uncovered about hope. Set your goals for what you want your life to be, determine a loving and giving path toward achieving your dreams, and believe in your future as you press onward through the difficulty. Peace, joy, and happiness will be yours. Believe it.

Have the Courage to Love

IF I COULD GIVE one directive in this book that had the power to change the lives of everyone, it would be for them to have the courage to love. I've written so many different ways a caregiver can love throughout this book and won't repeat them now. Just fix in your mind how significant it is to be able to truly love other people.

Caregivers, who valiantly do all they can to ease the pain and discomfort of their loved ones need to be honored for their courage. Somehow, they keep going amid their hardship and I salute them for having the courage to accomplish the difficult. Loving another to the point where the health and well-being of their disabled loved one is the major objective in life is hard. Offering your very best to one who cannot return the favor and sometimes to those who are unhappy, unappreciative, and angry requires great courage and love.

Loving yourself takes courage, too. It may seem selfish, but it is not. If you are not at the 'top of your game' neither will be your service for your loved one. It may not seem to require courage, but it does.

Caregivers need to ask the hard questions. Why don't I take better care of myself? What is holding me back? Taking better care of yourself may be a strong influence in ridding some of the other emotional concerns that you have. Only you can do this!

Taking care of yourself may mean having the courage to ask others for help. Nearly every internet home page of major health associations dealing with the emotional difficulties of caregiving, suggests caregivers, regardless of their natural reluctance, should be willing to ask for physical help when it is needed.

Asking for help is especially important when a caregiver faces a task or a treatment for which they haven't received the proper training to do. I am sure no medical professional expects caregivers to provide a service for which they have not been sufficiently educated. If you find yourself in this situation, it is your responsibility to speak up and let other people know. The information and training you need to make both you and your loved one safe and comfortable may only be a phone call away.

Caregivers give many reasons for not asking for help, but none of them can't be overcome. This is not only a matter of physical labor, but of preserving your own health and physical wellbeing. Studies reveal caregivers, on the average, die four years earlier than other adults who do not provide caregiving. 'Pick up the phone' and call for help. Wise caregivers who love themselves and thus truly love their disabled loved one will do so.

Having the courage to share your feelings is part of loving yourself, as well. For too long, caregivers have thought expressing their emotions and discussing their hardships to be disloyal to their loved ones or a sign of weakness. Exhaustion and loneliness can wear upon the strongest of caregivers who have the greatest intentions and unless you have the courage to share, you will undermine your own abilities and happiness.

Loving is a journey with happiness as its ultimate reward.

Love can change hearts and lives.

Have the Courage to Act

LET'S LOOK AT SOME men who did have the courage to act:

No one who saw the movie Schindler's List will ever forget the ending scene when Schindler is presented a letter signed by all of the 1,100 Jews he saved during the tragic period of the Third Reich in Germany. He kept repeating over and over "I could have saved so many more".

But the remaining leader of the factory employees reminded him that, because of Schindler's courage, in the face of Hitler's atrocities, generations to come would also be saved. The movie itself is a story of courage in humanity's darkest hour. The movie reminds us of the slogan therein, that "he who saves one life, saves the entire world."

Well, modern caregivers may not ever do something as extraordinary as the saving of the 1,100 Jews, but they can take humble pride in the improving or lengthening of one human life. By today' statistics, 44 million current caregivers and 10 million soon-to-be-caregivers will each have the privilege of improving another person's life just because they have or will have the courage to act.

John F. Kennedy said, "The courage of life is often less dramatic spectacle than the courage of a final moment; but it is no less a magnificent mixture of triumph and tragedy. A man does what he must— in spite of personal consequences, in spite of obstacles and dangers, and pressures — and that is the basis of all human morality." President Kennedy was one who knew how to seize the moment, particularly if it required personal courage.

Doing difficult things and making hard decisions requires courage at every level. It takes courage to use a new medical device, go through a new procedure, change your routine, or even increase your patient' physical therapy exercises. Having the courage to change and act is important. I'll never forget the 1989 image of a man, carrying two shopping bags and defying the tanks of Tiananmen Square. He became a global symbol of courage. He did what he thought was right in the face of great personal consequence. That took courage.

All of us have strong feelings about the right or the wrong of something. It might be discrimination, clean air, war, pristine parks, disagreeable political candidates, or the treatment of a loved one. Is there something holding you back from taking action?

Walt Disney said, "Courage is the main quality of leadership, in my opinion, no matter where it is exercised. Usually it implies some risk— especially in new undertakings." Walt Disney took many risks. It helped that he made good judgments, but he still was willing to step up and make the tough decisions.

One thing all of these men who had the courage to act have in common is they also had the courage to keep going despite challenging and in Schindler's case, horrifying circumstances.

Do you want to give up on the things that mean the most to you? Your health? Your marriage? Other relationships? Your finances? Your dreams. Your critical position as a caregiver? There are so many things we all struggle with, things that cause great anxiety either for a moment or for the long-term.

The feeling or temptation to quit during hard times strikes us all, even when giving up is not consistent with who we are. Take heart, those who persevere will win the reward.

As with each of these men, every person can have the courage to make a difference in their lives and the lives of another just by the choices he or she makes every day. We need to be willing to face situations and act, sometimes making hard choices for our loved one.

Don't forget the most important part of facing a situation is seeing beyond the circumstances. Setting goals not only provides us with an opportunity to self-reflect on our current status or problems and priorities, but also makes a vision of future happiness possible.

If you don't set objectives to reach a certain goal, how will you know when you get there?

FINAL COMMENTS ABOUT DEVELOPING COURAGE

THE BRITISH DICTIONARY SUGGESTS that courage is, *the power or quality of dealing with or facing danger, fear, pain, etc.* The courage of one's convictions is the confidence to act in accordance with one's beliefs."

So, I encourage you to have the courage to ask, believe, act and love. We are all capable of taking steps on this pathway to happiness without having to wait for someone else, or even for a miraculous event, because the strength and the miracle to change our lives lies within us.

You will discover each step you make brings confidence and worth. Your courage will give you mastery over your life, making hope and happiness and greater love for your loved one possible.

13.

THE SUCCESS

Pure love is a willingness to give without a thought of receiving anything in return.

– Peace Pilgrim

Stories of Constancy and Love

THE FOLLOWING SEVEN TRUE stories comprise a collective picture of what is right in a care giving relationship. The caregivers met the responsibilities of caring for their loved ones without suffering a loss of love. Their love grew stronger in the face of hardships. These caregivers found the happy side of caregiving and the joy of giving regardless of their frustrating circumstances. They never gave up seeking the best for their loved ones and in the process found strength, satisfaction and renewed love.

I am indebted to each of them who had the courage to share their personal stories. We need to hear more about these heroes who face the daily challenge of loving beyond all boundaries. I hope you can see their great strength and understand the happiness they hold can be yours.

Caregiver #1

THIS STORY CONCERNS A very special couple – the husband fighting for dignity and his wife fighting to preserve it for him. They are both professionals, who have always sought for excellence in their lives. Now they seek end of life happiness and understanding.

"We have been married for 53-½ years. I would say I have been a caregiver for my husband just about the last two to two and one-half years. I am now the primary decision maker, even the stronger partner in what used to be a primarily equal partnership.

My husband started developing dementia about five years ago. It began by losing the ability to reason/think logically and make decisions. He would ask simple questions, for example, "Which way should I go?" or "How do I send/forward this email?" I became worried about his driving. He was unwilling to recognize a problem, attributing lapses to "getting old".

We used to be really evenly matched playing games, especially word games, which we loved as we were both very competitive. Now I have to explain so many things, which he still cannot understand. This uneven ground that we are on has changed our relationship to some extent.

I feel that we are just beginning the experience with care giving. For the first couple of years he was still pretty independent, and his physical health is excellent, so I'm sure I haven't begun to experience my most difficult care giving experiences yet.

I think our hardest times are the times when my husband becomes angry or critical for something he perceives, but which has no basis in reality. It is so easy to react emotionally or become defensive, temporarily forgetting that he has a disease that has caused his behavior, and he is not responsible for his actions. He often apologizes later, as he himself cannot understand why he acted the way he did.

I think I am learning to be more compassionate, less critical. I feel bad that it has taken this situation for me to experience these qualities, but I am glad that I am now recognizing this. I feel such compassion when I see this formerly bright, decisive, quick thinking man unable to understand, not only how to use the TV remote, but unable to comprehend what it is for. It breaks my heart that he can't remember the names of our children or where they live. He was always so proud of his education at Columbia and NYU, and although he remembers the feeling that it was important, he doesn't know where he went or why.

I realize more and more how unimportant non-consequential things are. What he chooses to wear, how he makes his bed, where he puts things – these things really don't matter. They do not need to be corrected and certainly shouldn't be criticized.

Others who have helped are our children, my husband's siblings, and a few friends who recognize how important it is for me to have breaks and offer to spend time with him, without me.

I am fortunate in that my physical condition has not yet been affected, and my love for him is still intact. In a few years, I may look back and see things I don't recognize yet.

I have always believed that one of my best attributes was patience. However, I am learning to see patience differently. I have always needed to be busy and accomplishing something. It has been (and still is) hard for me to slow down and spend time just "being". I keep thinking of the movie "The Notebook", and remembering how that husband read the same thing to his wife day after day.

I can foresee my husband needing more and more of my time as he is unable to entertain himself and I know that I need to slow down and take time to do things with him. This will require a different form of patience than I have ever experienced and that I can see will be much more difficult for me.

I think this emphasizes the big difference between someone who needs physical care but is mentally alert, and someone who is physically capable, but doesn't function well mentally and emotionally. It seems like the demand on the caregiver is very different in these two cases.

What I need the most now is for people who would like to spend time with my husband (friends, siblings, children or grandchildren) to include him in activities – walks, lunch, kid's games, etc. That is occurring to some extent; but I understand that people are busy and often just don't think about it.

I still work part time; usually about ½ day a week, and am becoming increasingly nervous about leaving him alone. Our children have been trying to help out when they can. I may have to quit, but I feel that it is a good outlet for me to stay involved in something outside my home. This may sound naïve or unrealistic, but I have never been a worrier, and I still don't worry. I believe that everything will always work out. I consistently feel so blessed that I cannot justify worrying about things that may never happen. There really is nothing that I worry about on a long-term basis.

Caregiver #2

A GOOD FRIEND LOST his wife to ALS (Lou Gehrigs' Disease), a tragic and terrible disease. He is a very precise person and made extensive notes about his experience. We knew his wife and knew how he loved her. This is his story about those last 53 weeks:

My wife's first symptom of worry came in the fall and winter of 1999, when her left leg would not respond properly. During January, four tests failed to establish a positive diagnosis. Then in February she tested positive for ALS. Other tests confirmed the earlier diagnosis that month. She fell on a trip to Arizona, leading up to the eventual use of a cane, commencing in March. However, the disease was advancing so rapidly that by March 23 she was unable to even use a cane, and began using a walker.

By April 17 neither of her legs would move. By May 15 her weight was down to 119 lbs. and her breathing was 106%. By June 5 her breathing would be down to 78%. In early August, an elevator was installed to help her mobility. We made a move to ease her travel and breathing was now down to 60% by September. By November she had lost 85% of her speech.

In December, we moved back to our home. That ride would be her last time in a car. Her breathing then was 27%. On New Year's Day, 2001, looking forward, the prospects for the New Year were no better than the extremely difficult year of 2000. By early January she cannot swallow her pills, drinks from a syringe, and is eating less at all meals. In early February, she develops bed sores. By mid-February she is in a coma, needing physical assistance for everything. Morphine is given regularly to ease the pain. Feb 14 with the nurse there, she has hardly any pulse, blood pressure is 70/40 and bed sores are evident when we rolled her on to her side. She was then helped on to her back again where she breathed twice and passed away after fighting a gallant and mostly positive fight.

I was mentally and physically exhausted. It was a terrible year. Clearly the worst 53 weeks of my life. After the funeral when everyone was finally gone I started remembering the good things. Our morning rituals, we continued to laugh through the difficulties, enjoyed good music and good books. We openly discussed the disease with each other and with the family.

We tried to do as many normal things as possible. We wrote lots of positive letters and video tapes. We worked very hard at keeping a positive attitude. I admired her ability to do that.

I discovered early on that the caregiver is really in charge, but I discussed everything with her. There were so many medical issues, each requiring a discussion and a decision. We found out that the disease robbed us of our strength—both of us. We were exhausted by bedtime every evening. As a caregiver, I found that I could not get sick. I did hurt my back through all of the lifting. I found that a hurt back needs a rest. But despite the pain and difficulty, our love made the lifting easier.

Caregiver #3

THIS CAREGIVER HAS BEEN providing care to his wife for decades. Both of their attitudes have made it possible to function as well as they seem to according to the comments below. I know them and believe the comments made are very illustrative of their admirable lives.

Our relationship is quite excellent. We are kind and courteous to each other. We are still expressing our love to each other. We are civil and very good friends. I don't know what I expected, but I didn't expect things to be so good. We enjoy being together and still share many important things.

I give my wife much of the credit for our relationship. During the tough years when teenagers were acting out and we had financial struggles, she remained constant. She never wavered. It gave me the courage and determination to do the same. I believe we both worked hard at building a strong marriage and a happy relationship. As corny as it might sound, we loved each other enough to make it work.

Going to the hospital was the worst. It is easy to think about things that are the worst. I tried not to do that. I had a fairly high degree of faith that we were being watched over. That helped me. I always wondered when she was ill, why the physician would send her to the hospital. I wondered if there were other adjustments that would also help. The only other negative thing was her sometime unwillingness to take medicine or comply with the physician's instructions.

Our best times were when we were working together. I was being patient, kindly and   compassionate, and she was responsive, predictable, and pleasant. I appreciated her sense of humor, even in the toughest of times. Her positive acceptance of what I was trying to do encouraged me to try harder, to seek to be better, and to be kinder in all that I did for her.

I believe that I have never stopped seeing her as she had always been – alive, smart, fun, dynamic and loving. I don't believe I ever saw her as someone less than she was.

I really believe that my love for my wife has increased, not decreased, during our care giving. I have grown closer to her as I have provided assistance and care. While I believe we both have worked at it, something positive has come from my care giving.

I have learned not to repeat, not to call her when she repeats, to treat her with love and respect, not to over-react, not to ignore her or consider her opinions of lessening value. I would very much want to see her health and motivation improve. Since that is not very likely I am trying to make her life the best it can be. We have not yet sought outside assistance. I hope we will never have to.

I worry most about having sufficient financial resources for her end of life medical expenses. I have heard some pretty horrific stories about costs. Fortunately, we don't have unresolved issues. We discuss pretty much everything. We have talked quite a bit about what happens when one of us dies. Fortunately, we really have no disagreements on end of life issues, nor any other matter. Because of our love, we attempt to add to each other' life with kindness. I believe we are succeeding.

Caregiver #4

THIS IS THE STORY of someone I respect and admire a great deal. She has nursed and cared for her husband with remarkable tenderness and concern. Her husband's ordeal through multiple operations has tired her but not discouraged her. She includes below how their love has enabled them to sustain one another through countless discouraging moments.

To begin with, there is great irony in the fact that I have ended up a "caregiver". I have always had an extreme aversion to anything involving blood or anything icky! (When our youngest daughter announced, years ago, that she was going into nursing, I questioned how she could really be my daughter.)

It has actually been easier for me to adjust to the time and energy required in being a caregiver than it has been in learning to deal with the medical treatments that are required. I believe there must have been some divine intervention involved in my developing the ability to provide all the treatments necessary for my husband's recovery. Apparently almost anybody can adjust to doing whatever is necessary under difficult circumstances.

I do agree with what has been written about the importance of love. Without love, this job would be nearly impossible, especially if it is on a long-term basis. I feel very fortunate and blessed that I still love my husband and enjoy his company after nearly 60 years of marriage.

Our circumstances have been made easier by the decisions we made early on as his health issues developed. We agreed to "take it one day at a time", and to "keep the eternal perspective.

Our social life is necessarily very limited now. However, we have been blessed with a wonderful family who are living very active and interesting lives that we are able to enjoy vicariously. We are able to spend time with many of them, and those we don't see often keep us updated on Instagram, etc. Reminiscing about our own lifetime experiences is also enjoyable and important to us. The point I am trying to make is that there is no reason to be bored or miserable when your life' circumstances require you to drastically change your lifestyle. Reading is my favorite pastime and my current limitations have allowed me more time to read. It gives me something to look forward to at the end of a busy day or while waiting in different medical facilities for the many doctor appointments my husband necessarily has.

We believe that God gives us challenges to test us, and He also gives us the wisdom and strength to handle those challenges if we ask for His help.

Another thing that has made it easier for both of us is that we both have a healthy sense of humor, and so far, we have been able to keep it. If we lose that, we will know we are in trouble!

Caregiver #5

THE STORY OF CAREGIVER #5 is tender and touching. It tells the story of another friend who has spent a major part of her life facing the trials of a difficult marriage and the stress and frustration of a near impossible caregiving responsibility. She is a wonderful person and a loyal and loving human being. You will find hope in her endurance and determination.

I'm married, my husband and I celebrated 40 years of marriage in June. My husband has been in a care center for five years. He has Huntington's disease. It is a neurological disease – the neurons in his brain are dying. The disease has been compared to Alzheimer's, MS and Parkinson's diseases, simultaneously all wrapped up in one. It destroys the ability to reason, communicate and to focus. It can affect males or females. You have a 50-50 chance of it affecting the next generation.

When my husband found out he first told his family before he told me and then pulled his three sons together to let them know he had what Grandma H. had. It was told to them that it was our hope that they did not have children because the only way to break the cycle is not to have children.

Our sons were 18, 16, and 12. I told him that they could and should make their choices for themselves when that time came. He told them he didn't know how long before the disease forced him to retire. For the next several years – except for that day when he talked to the boys – he didn't speak about HD to the boys again. I was the one who dealt with what he had told them. The younger son was more affected and worried. He was concerned that he would get HD.

The next years were hard with him because he was making rash decisions and purchases. I came home to new cars in the garage, snowmobiles, etc. He was OCD when it came to the boys mowing the lawn, it had to be cut in a specific order. The air conditioner had to be turned up to 80 degrees before it would come on. Shoveling snow had to be done a certain way. He would take off for a bike ride not letting anyone know where he was going. He would get up early in the morning and ride his bike in the dark. He would wear dark clothing on a busy street at 4:30 – 5:00 am. It was useless trying to reason with him.

When it was getting known that he would need to retire I decided that I needed to stop working so that I could kind of know where he would be. I didn't want anyone to come to me and say when he walked, his balance was not good – a typical reaction to that disease.

Shortly after he retired he couldn't drive anymore. A neighbor was going to take him to lunch one day. At that time, our son and his family were living with us. My granddaughter was 18 months and my grandson was three. I had to run an errand and when I got home, I could not find my husband. I found him in the bedroom with a gun in his hand. He said he had purchased the gun while he was working. I took the gun from him because I had the 18-month-old in my arms. At the time, I didn't know there was a bullet in the chamber.

His walking was getting more unstable. We got him a walking stick but he wouldn't always use it and a phone with a push button to get me. Those two items needed to go with him when he walked. He was not a fan of doing it. We had to set boundaries. One day he fell off the front porch and broke his hip. It was then necessary to seek additional help. I found a facility that would take him part-time. Jim was so difficult to help, and they could handle him better and he would do what they asked of him.

Looking back now, I can see how hard it was for him. He was in his 50's and was losing his independence and had to have help to do most things. In addition, it was like dealing with a man acting like a child. I continue to be the 'bad guy' who prevents him from doing many of the things he wants to do.

In 2011, I went to the doctor for a checkup. It turned out something was not right. I failed a stress test and because of the concerning results of an angiogram I was told that I could be walking and just drop over. That caused the boys to insist that we put Jim in the care facility full-time. I could visit regularly, although with great difficulty because of this attitude and conduct.

He eventually had another accident and broke the other hip which confined him permanently to a wheelchair. I am so pleased that the care facility has taken so good care of him, wheelchair and all.

Early on it was hard to love someone who had his own set of rules to live by and would not bend or compromise. It had to be his way at all times. There were many times that I thought about leaving him. But I didn't, I've stuck by him. I married him for forever. It would have been easy to say I'm out of here, but I still love the man. My oldest son asked why I didn't just divorce him. I said you just don't do that, it's not that easy.

When I see him now and the condition he's in, my heart hurts for him and I'm his greatest advocate while trying to make sure he is well taken care of. I have sympathy for him and pray that one day Heavenly Father will call him home and he will be freed from the trapped body he is in.

Life is not easy. Caregiving is not easy. I have guilt when I think of my feelings regarding cleaning up messes on the carpets, walls, furniture and him. It was not my finest moment. I have had to come to a place where I am still caregiving. But, I'm a better caregiver now because I still need to look out for his needs and care. Fortunately, the nursing staff is able to handle his outbursts.

I have been a married "widow" for a long time. I would love to have someone say let me help you, let me worry about this or that. I feel weighted down with how I am going to pay for his care and will the stress and anxiety kill me. This isn't just Jim's journey. I need to show that I have been on the same journey. My faith is my anchor and I know that Heavenly Father knows what is best for each of us, and one day he will call Jim home, enabling him to soar once more. As for me, I have had wonderful people put in my path to help me along this journey. Thank you for letting me tell a part of my story.

<u>Caregiver #6</u>

THE STORY OF CAREGIVER #6 was written by Louise Penney, a mystery writer, regarding her husband, Michael. The story below is a condensed version of the story that appeared in the October/November 2016 issue of the AARP Magazine. It is a story of love, waiting, and correct caregiving attitudes:

The Doctor did not bother with niceties or try to cushion the blow. My husband had dementia. And it seemed to be moving quickly . . . I took his hand and held it as the doctor went through the options. It didn't take long. There was none.

. . . And I learned that my day, my happiness, decided by how Michael was doing, I needed to make it about how I was doing. How well I was accepting, adjusting and looking ahead. Seeing issues before they arose . . . Michael can no longer walk. He's in a wheelchair and needs a lift to get out of bed. He needs to be cleaned and dressed and fed. But he remains what he always was - the happiest man in any room.

And I've found no small measure of happiness, too - and gratitude. I am pleased that I'm younger than he is, and had the strength and energy to care for him. We are fortunate that we have such great friends. I am happy that I work from home and that we have the resources to look after him.

I'm grateful that the dementia did not make him angry or abusive. I'm grateful that I love him so much. Looking after someone with dementia whom you don't like would be hell. And I'm grateful that I'm losing him this way, slowly. We get to live our lives fully, right to the end. Of course, our idea of "fully" has evolved, too.

Our lives are full of kindness, of friendship, of love. There is clarity now, and simplicity. He rarely speaks and no longer knows my name. I think he smiles more broadly when he sees me, but it's possible that my well of wishful thinking hasn't quite run dry.

Michael is not in pain. He is not anxious or afraid. I am, sometimes, but he is not. I cry a lot, I miss him so much - the companionship, the ease and the thoughtful conversations. I miss someone to travel with, and have dinners out with – and someone to discuss the day with.

I miss the deep hugs.

I miss being loved

I am often lonely, and exhausted, and feel not quite adequate. I want it to be over. And dread the day that it is.

Sometimes I can't recall what Michael was like, before. I can look at photos of him and smile, but sight of his handwriting reduces me to tears. Fortunately, most of the time, though, I am content, at peace . . .

A friend put it so beautifully. Michael is simply losing altitude. I have promised myself that when he touches down, he'll be at home. Here, with me, holding his hand.

Caregiver #7

THE STORY OF CAREGIVER #7 is an inspiration. Contrary to most of the other stories, this is written by the patient. She illuminates how a married couple can remain strong through personal trauma and then, discovering strengths and new determination, together they care for others.

You're alone, and trying to care for two parents every need, and your own family. Your family-siblings and friends have moved on to their own things. You are stalled on care mode, and no one seems to realize, you might have needs. You even begin to lose your health. Some friends seem to condemn you if you speak about hard issues and that you are having a hard time handling, what seems like almost everything . . . or so it seems.

Friends want happy, laughter, and care free. But, you're not free, and you won't just put parents in an institution, visit once in a while, leave and go live your life. You can lose your friends, even invites that could bring a little relief. But, they seem absorbed in their own social life, and besides you're no longer fitting. You find yourself very alone . . .

Thank God for a good spouse. Not perfect, they get tired also, but they don't walk away in the midst of what seems overwhelming, they are faithful . . . it has taken several years, driving eight hours to a specialist MD, to know the many tests needed, to begin to repair my health. My mother put into me to reach out and care for others, literally. Overseas part time, helping poor, homeless. So, how could I turn from my parents, and not care for them. I grieved quite easy, and had a peace for being there, doing the best I could. Then came my husband's parents with Alzheimer and cancer (like my parents) I had learned, and was prepared to lift up, and carry my husband thru. I knew the pitfalls of personal involvement, and holding strong.

FINAL COMMENTS ABOUT
<u>GETTING IT RIGHT</u>

THERE ARE MANY FAITHFUL, loving caregivers who devote their time and energy to the welfare and well-being of injured or ill loved ones. Many sacrifice so much that their health deteriorates, but they carry on because they know they should. Their love for the one who is ill gets them through. They are the heroes of care giving. They give because they should, and they give because they love someone dear to them.

14.

THE CONCLUSION

Never be afraid to do the things that make you feel free.
– PURELOVEQUOTES.COM

Take Charge of Your Life No Matter How You Feel or What You Are Feeling.

HOW YOU FEEL MATTERS, but it should not be the compass directing your life. While the focus of other chapters is on the circumstances of your relationship with your patient and what you can do about it, this chapter centers on you, the caregiver.

What do you do with your feelings in the caregiving situation? For there will be many different emotions. Some will be good, and some will be very destructive and you can't ignore the negative ones or they will destroy you. You must face your inner demons and conquer them on a regular basis, or you will become mired in a vicious cycle of frustration and hopelessness.

Having a realistic outlook on your emotions isn't a negative thing. So, let's get them all out in the open. Believing your feelings will fall in line with your responsibilities and goals without great struggle would be naïve and foolish.

Those in a caregiving situation have a responsibility to identify what is causing negative feelings to arise, and search for the tools to "fix" the problem before it can poison their lives. Gaining a clear perspective about your emotions will challenge you, but will free you to experience happiness in your life.

So, dig deep as we examine feelings: how they affect your life and how to gain a new perspective on them.

What do you feel about yourself?

Take out a piece of paper and pen and let's go to work. Make two columns. At the top of one write Happiness and at the top of the other column write Sorrow. Begin with the first column. List all of the people, things and events you know that bring you joy, friendship and companionship. Remember spouse, family, neighbors and friends. Also, consider your employment, your recreation, skills, pleasures, motivations, peace of mind, religion, country, freedom, etc.

In the Sorrow column, list all of the things that are currently troubling you. Things like your negative feelings for care giving, loneliness, fatigue, frustration, anger, regret, confusion, relationships, friendships, family, abandonment, entrapment, escape, self-confidence, etc.

This list will require complete honesty. Sometimes things bother us in a way we are reluctant to admit. This is the time to develop a plan for real happiness and love, and it begins by being honest with everything you feel, both positive and negative.

Once you have listed your feelings, take out another sheet and prioritize both columns. Descend each list from the most influential at the top of the columns to the least influential at the bottom of the columns.

Now step away from the two lists. Leave them for at least a couple of hours, or even a few days. When you return to the lists, determine if the priorities are still correct.

Your first assignment with this list is to do something to increase your appreciation for, or show your appreciation of the top item in your Happiness column. Remember, who or what is the most important person, thing or event in your life. Hopefully, your loved one will be high on that list. After deciding what could or should be done, do it quickly.

Next, pick the top entry on your Sorrow column and take action to minimize, control, or eliminate the disruptive effect that negative has on your life and the feelings it generates.

As you keep moving forward with each thing on your list, you will build up positive feelings in your life and diminish negative ones. The negatives will never disappear, because we all have thorns amid life's roses, but they can be contained. Your actions will determine whether the Happiness Column or the Sorrow Column rules your life.

Do this on a regular basis by making new lists when your older list changes. You'll be surprised at the shifts in perspective you will make and the emotional maturity you will gain.

Do this same exercise for how you feel about your loved one, and another list about caretaking. Then take action. Do things to feed the positives and to minimize the negatives. Be honest, and include your feelings about your role as a caretaker and how you feel about an increase or a decrease in your responsibilities.

Your feelings really do matter, but they can be controlled and changed if needed. Don't let negative thoughts and feelings drive your life to disaster. Instead, overcome them with love and positive actions. Make your journey one to happiness.

There is one last subject, every caregiver must dig deep for and must prepare to face.

You will not be a caregiver forever. The day will come when your ill loved one passes on.

Where will you be then?

If you are wise, you will take that reality into consideration. Are you making the decisions for quality time with your loved one now, so you will have no regrets then? Are you keeping your circle of support wide enough now, so you will not be stranded on a deserted island later?

Your eventual happiness and success might just depend on the planning that you do now. Look at and answer these questions, because if there are feelings you need to change, now is the time to change them:

Will you have to overcome the feelings of aloneness?

What will be needed to sufficiently regain your physical strength?

How will you manage to eliminate the feelings of frustration?

Will you need to grieve after the loved one is gone?

Will it be necessary to forgive your loved one?

Will you be able to forgive yourself for negative thoughts?

Will you feel free from any other emotional baggage?

Will you have the courage to be happy – again?

Will you be able to experience love - again?

Will you look forward to a new and less burdened existence?

By examining your feelings and asking hard questions about your life and your future, you can truly be free to love and pave a pathway to happiness in your life. Having a very successful and meaningful caregiving experience doesn't happen by accident, but by design.

You choose.

This last chapter concludes by taking these words of counsel from another website

Care Giver Self Advocacy Messages to Live By: *Choose to take charge of your life. We fall into caregiving often because of an unexpected event, but somewhere along the line you need to step back and consciously say, "I choose to take on this caregiving role."*

It goes a long way toward eliminating the feeling of being a victim. Love, honor and value yourself. Self-care isn't a luxury. It is your right as a human being. Step back and recognize just how extraordinary you are, and remember your own good health, emotional and physical, is one of the most meaningful and best presents you can give your loved one patient. Seek, accept and at times demand help. Caregiving, especially at its most intense levels, is definitely more than a one-person job."

Stand up and be counted. Recognize that caregiving comes on top of being a parent, a child, a spouse. Honor your caregiving role and speak up for your well, deserved recognition and rights. That can be done without withdrawing your love and caring for your loved one. Become your own advocate, both within your own immediate caregiving sphere and beyond.

This is good advice to take heart for the future can be bright. There are definite solutions and steps to be taken to make caregiving a success, an act of kindness and love, and still be accomplished by taking care of both you and your patient with love the guiding influence.

Love can be found and not lost.

AUTHOR'S CONCLUSION

WHEN I FINISHED THIS book, I asked myself "if there is one thing I wish the readers would take away from reading it, what would it be". I thought about that, because many important concepts had been presented. It was not difficult! It was that *everyone deserves to be loved*. Everyone deserves to feel the joy and sensation of someone else caring for them, really caring for and loving them. That means everyone including caregivers and those blessed to receive their care.

Being loved and giving love are eternal principles. That must mean that everything began with love and will eventually end with love. So, it all begins with service which is really charity. Next comes demonstrating through charity your love for your patient, and loving others to bring about real hope and happiness. Then you can discover there really is a sure path to happiness, true happiness. That path is clearly love.

RESOURCES

FAMILY CAREGIVERS ARE OFTEN over-burdened and under-informed: they need access to the best care giving resources to support them in the caregiver role. We are indebted to the *American Society for Aging* for the following list of helpful care giving resources. (14)

1.   **AARP**

AARP's Caregiving Resource Center provides family caregivers with information, tools and resources to help them on their care giving journey. The site also provides access to care giving experts in various issue areas, who provide information through blogs, webinars and one-on-one interaction through social media channels. Family members and friends can find a supportive online community that offers a safe space to connect with others experiencing similar challenges as they care for a loved one.

2.   **ALZHEIMER'S ASSOCIATION**

Specializing in caring for those with Alzheimer's and other dementias, the Alzheimer's Association has links with details on what to expect for each disease stage. It also explains behaviors specific to Alzheimer's and links caregivers to local respite care and activities, legal and financial advice and resources, and local caregiver support groups. Also included are pragmatic stress tests and caregiver message boards.

3.   ALZHEIMER'S FOUNDATION

The Alzheimer's Foundation provides online tips, a toll-free hotline, educational and social services, professional development, advocacy and grants, as well as a link for teens to connect, educate others and support care giving teens. The Foundation puts its stamp of approval on facilities that meet their strenuous standards for good care for those with Alzheimer's, hosts a national memory screening day and a national brain game challenge.

4.   AMERICAN ASSOCIATION OF CAREGIVING YOUTH

The American Association of Caregiving Youth is geared toward supporting the 1.4 million children and teens who are care giving for parents and grandparents. They provide counseling and support services, education and advocacy. The Association works directly with schools to help students remain academically successful while they are in the caregiving role.

5.   ARCH NATIONAL RESPITE NETWORK

The ARCH (Access to Respite Care and Help) National Respite Network connects caregivers directly to local respite and crisis care services, assists and promotes the development of quality respite and crisis care programs, and advocates for respite in all forums.

6.   CAREGIVER ACTION NETWORK

The Caregiver Action Network (CAN) (formerly the National Family Caregivers Association) offers practical lists for immediate help with caregiving: patient file checklist, doctors office checklist, how to find a support group, medication checklist, independent living assessment and helpful videos. This easy-to-navigate site takes caregivers through step-by-step processes to help get a handle on care giving.

7.   CAREGIVER SUPPORT SERVICES
       Caregiver Support Services supports family and professional caregivers through direct services such as trainings on medication, on how to become a personal assistant or a nursing assistant, case management, employee assistance, Alzheimer's and HIV/AIDS, as well as self-advocacy and other pertinent services.

8.   CARING.COM
       This website offers informative articles about common care giving concerns for family caregivers, and hosts a directory of services.

9.   CARING BRIDGE
       CaringBridge.org connects families and friends who are experiencing a significant health challenge through private websites where people can share updates and support.

10.   E CARE DIARY
       E Care Diary provides the tools and resources to simplify care giving, including the Care Diary, a medication- and appointment-management tool that helps families store and share their loved ones' information in a secure, private place.

11. ELDERCARE LOCATOR

A free nationwide directory assistance service, *eldercare* locator helps older persons and their family caregivers locate local support resources. It is administered through the National Association of Area Agencies on Aging in Washington, D.C.

12. FAMILY CAREGIVER ALLIANCE

The Family Caregiver Alliance supports caregivers through information, education, services and research. It also advocates for family caregivers, including a new initiative to foster a consumer movement to improve healthcare quality, coordination and communication for elders and their caregivers. FCA also connects caregivers to services and support groups and has an ongoing story project. FCA's National Center on Caregiving advances the development of high-quality, cost effective policies and programs for caregivers in every state. The Family Care Navigator is a state-by-state, online guide to help families locate government, nonprofit and private caregiver support programs.

13. HOME INSTEAD SENIOR CARE

To hire trusted care for a loved one in your home, the Home Instead Senior Care network of locally owned franchises has been providing in-home care for elders since 1994, so older adults can age in their home, and caregivers can get a well-earned break. For either a few hours a day or 24-hour care, Home Instead's caregivers are screened, trained, insured and bonded.

14.   LOTSA HELPING HANDS

Through Lotsa Helping Hands anyone can create private Web-based communities to organize care and help for people in need, with a group calendar for scheduling and sign-ups for tasks from providing respite to meals, rides and visits. There is a place for announcements, a message board and an information section for families to store and retrieve health data, emergency contacts, medications and legal and financial records for designated members.

15.   I'M A CAREGIVER/MEDICARE.GOV

The Medicare.gov landing page for caregivers has resources, stories and newsletters about taking care of someone on Medicare. There are easy links to find out if procedures are covered, as well as finding someone to talk to about a multitude of potential nuts-and-bolts questions, from coverage to urgent care to complaints on kidney dialysis.

16.   NATIONAL ALLIANCE FOR CAREGIVING

A coalition of 40 national organizations that conducts research and policy analysis, develops national programs and works to increase public awareness of family caregiving issues across the life span.

17.   NATIONAL ADULT DAY SERVICES ASSOCIATION

The National Adult Day Services association connects family caregivers with adult day centers and supports the interests of adult day services' providers. It provides members with advocacy, educational and networking opportunities, technical assistance and research, and communications services.

18. NATIONAL ASSOCIATION OF PROFESSIONAL GERIATRIC CARE MANAGERS

The National Association of Professional Geriatric Care Managers is a nonprofit professional development organization whose mission is to advance professional geriatric care management through education, collaboration and leadership. Members are also listed on the site, where they can be linked to caregivers. The site explains care management and how to finding the best geriatric care manager, and offers easy links for families to search for one via zip code.

19. NATIONAL FAMILY CAREGIVER SUPPORT PROGRAM

The National Family Caregiver Support Program provides grants to states and territories, based on their share of the population ages 70 and older, to fund a range of supports that help family and informal caregivers to care for their loved one at home for as long as possible. Overseen by the Administration on Aging, the NFCSP provides five types of services: information to caregivers about available services, assistance to caregivers in gaining access to the services, individual counseling, organization of support groups, and caregiver training, respite care, and supplemental services, on a limited basis. These services work with other state- and community-based services to provide a coordinated set of supports for caregivers.

20.   NATIONAL INSTITUTE ON AGING'S NATIONAL
       ALZHEIMER'S EDUCATION AND REFERRAL CENTER
       The National Institute on Aging's National Alzheimer's Ed-
       ucation and Referral Center has a section for Caregivers with
       tip sheets and resources on behaviors, care, communication,
       relationships, safety, caregiver health, legal and financial issue
       and stages. It has an extensive list of publications on caregiving
       and papers on the latest in Alzheimer's research. And there's
       an easy-to-navigate, thorough and helpful Frequently Asked
       Questions section.

21.   NATIONAL LONG-TERM CARE CLEARINGHOUSE
       For caregivers or elders considering long-term care, this
       clearinghouse run by the Administration on Aging answers
       questions about the nature of long-term care, who needs it,
       how much it costs (with a state-by state breakdown), how it
       can be paid for, who provides care within long-term care facil-
       ities, details on Medicare and Medicaid coverage of long-term
       care, even legal help for LGBT elders considering long-term
       care. Not only does the site explain why everyone needs to plan
       for long-term care, but also it takes one through the step-by-
       step process.

22.   NEXT STEP IN CARE: FAMILY CAREGIVERS AND
       HEALTH CARE PROFESSIONALS WORKING TOGETHER
       United Hospital Fund's Next Step in Care program pro-
       vides information and advice to help family caregivers and
       healthcare providers plan safe and smooth transitions for pa-
       tients between care settings. All materials for family caregivers

are available in English, Spanish, Russian and traditional Chinese, and they emphasize careful planning, clear communication and ongoing care coordination.

23.   Rosalynn Carter Institute for Caregiving

The Rosalynn Carter Institute for Caregiving is an advocacy, education, research and service unit of Georgia Southwestern State University. It has its own training center, caregiving management certificate program, scholarship and fellowship opportunities, as well as caregiver resources.

24.   VA Caregiver Support

Run by the U.S. Department of Veterans Affairs, it provides support and services for family caregivers of veterans.

25.   Well Spouse Association

The Well Spouse Association provides peer support and education about the special challenges and unique issues facing "well" spouses. Members speak out on their care giving situations, providing a window into the not-so-well-known world of the estimated 16 million spousal caregivers in America and many more around the world.

COMING SOON
CAREGIVER SHORT BOOK 2

100 WAYS CAREGIVERS SURVIVE

THIS ENGAGING BOOK IS a survival workbook for all caregivers who seek relief from emotional pressures and a pathway to success and happiness. This short book contains 100 issues. One or more of these issues confront every current caregiver. The book dissects nearly all emotions now troubling caregivers and points the way to 100 tested solutions.

This informative book tells the story of how each of these stresses creates an emotional and physical roller coaster that prevents caregivers from being happy. It uncovers how loneliness, fatigue, frustration, entrapment, anger, guilt, loss of love, and many other troubling emotions can engulf a caregiver and preoccupy time, effort and commitment. A must read for all caregivers.

Other Caregiver Short Books to come are:
THE SURE PATH TO HOPE AND HAPPINESS
WINNING THE BATTLE OF CAREGIVER STRESS
WHY DON'T WE TALK ABOUT END-OF-LIFE?

INDEX AND REFERENCES

1   http://www.caregivers.com/blog/2012/07/caregiver-to-your-spouse/

2.   Wikipedia https://en.wikipedia.org/wiki/Hope

3.   *When A Spouse Dies* by Barbara R. Wheeler, DSW

4.   Wiki HowTo. http://www.wikihow.com/Love-Unconditionally

5.   *Huffington Post* -http://www.huffingtonpost.com/darryl-a-cob-bin/4-reasons-to-stay-married_b_4214293.html

6.   *Caregiving in the U.S.* 2015, done jointly by the National Alliance for Caregiving and the AARP Public Policy Institute

7.   http://www.goodreads.com/quotes/tag/truth-telling

8.   http://www.wikihow.com/Have-Hope

9.   *Huffington Post* http://www.huffingtonpost.com/tiffany-aliche/how-to-remain-hopefulin_b_8020294.html

10.   President Dieter F. Uchtdorf –https://www.lds.org/generalcon-ference/2008/10/the-infinite -power-of-hope?lang=eng

11.   http://www.wikihow.com/Eliminate-Guilt

12.   *Merriam–Webster* – http://www.merriam-webster.com/dictionary/hope

13.   *Jesus the Christ*, by James E. Talmage

14.   American Society of Aging – http://www.asaging.org/blog/25-organizations-take-care-caregivers

15.   https://www.brainyquote.com/quotes/topics/topic_happiness.html

16.   *New York Times*–http://www.nytimes.com/2013/12/15/opinion/sunday/a-formula-for-happiness.html

17.   *Huffington Post* –http://www.huffingtonpost.com/dr-carol-morgan/16-characteristics-of-real-love_b_6237802.html

18.   https://www.lds.org/general-conference/2016/10/abide-in-my-love?lang=eng

19.   http://www.strengthforthemoment.com/stories-of-caring/happiness-in-overcoming- and-giving/

20.   http://lonerwolf.com/different-types- of-love/

www.ingramcontent.com/pod-product-compliance
Lightning Source LLC
LaVergne TN
LVHW041219080426
835508LV00011B/1007